I DID NOT WANT TO LET YOU GO

A Widow's Walk with God

Mary Emma Tisinger

Carpenter's Son Publishing

Published by Carpenter's Son Publishing, Franklin, Tennessee

Scriptures marked KJV are taken from the
KING JAMES VERSION (KJV): public domain.

Scripture taken from THE HOLY BIBLE, NEW INTERNATIONAL VERSION®, NIV® Copyright © 1973, 1978, 1984, 2011 by Biblica, Inc.™ Used by permission. All rights reserved worldwide.

Edited by Robert Irvin

Cover and Interior Design by Suzanne Lawing

Printed in the United States of America

978-1-954437-89-0

I DID NOT WANT TO
LET YOU GO

COLD, THE WIND

I heard the rapping at the door
that cold December day;
I did not want to let you go.

Persistent, though,
Death came right in
and hastened you away.

Cold, cold the wind
above you now;
my heart, as well.

I dare not think ahead . . .
No more to hear your voice,
your laugh;

no more to see you smile,
or welcome me
at morning's dawn;

no more to say
good night.
For you have gone,

and cold, the wind;
cold, my lonely
heart.

A NOTE FROM THE AUTHOR

"It's just easier to leave than be left . . ."
The Story Within by Laura Oliver

Those of us who have lost someone we love to death can certainly attest to the truth of these words: "It's just easier to leave than be left . . . " At some point in each of our lives, death becomes a reality and we become "the one who is left."

Then we must begin the difficult journey from brokenness back to wholeness. Most find this journey an extremely painful one—but with God there is hope and healing.

Dark was the place in which I found myself the day my husband died. It was a terrible place, a place it seemed the sun could not reach, a place lonely and desolate. And great was my pain. In the following pages I invite you, the reader, to walk with me on my journey. Witness my struggle through the rocks at the bottom of the deep ravine into which I tumbled. But more important, witness that I did not walk alone—the Lord walked with me.

As He did for me, He can do for all who find themselves as "the one who is left."

In the following pages, I pray . . .
those who journey with me
find comfort and hope.

CONTENTS

PART V
The End Of The Road

PART VI
Adjustment

PART VII
Beginning Anew

PART VIII
Life Goes On

PART I

TO SLEEP, PERCHANCE TO DREAM

*For God does speak—now one way,
now another—though man may not
perceive it. In a dream, in a vision of
the night, when deep sleep falls . . .*

JOB 33:14, 15 (NIV)

THE DREAM

It was Ty! Finally, I had found him!

I had been searching everywhere for my husband. He had been away for a long time. Where? I did not know.

I ran to him, excited; so glad to see him. But . . . where was that big hug I was expecting? He held his arms straight out to the side, shoulder level, stiff and robot-straight, refusing to touch me.

Was he trying to keep distance between us?

Then . . . he sat in a chair. I moved over and sat on his lap. I wanted so much to feel his arms around me, holding me tight. But again, he held his arms out to the side, shoulder level, stiff and straight.

"Put your arms around me, Ty. Hold me," I managed to say. Sadness filled his eyes, but he did not speak. And he did not move.

"Put your arms around me, please," I repeated. "I need you to hold me."

Nothing changed. He continued to hold his arms straight to the side, shoulder level, stiff and straight.

Finally, with a sad, almost pitying look in his eyes, he said, "I can't."

Shocked, I moved away. Why? Why couldn't he put his arms around me and hold me?

Was there someone else? There must be . . .

Just then, the ceiling fan above the bed caught my attention . . . It was only a dream.

SNAPSHOT

"To sleep . . . perchance to dream . . . "

Shakespeare's words—so well-known to students everywhere—took on special significance for me after my husband's death. To sleep became especially difficult, and to dream seemed just as elusive. I longed to dream of my husband Ty. I yearned for anything that would help me feel him close again. But many of my nights were relatively sleepless, and my dreams were few. Being alone can be extremely difficult to face after fifty-plus years of sharing life with someone you love, knowing that suddenly he or she is gone.

Several years have gone by since my husband's death. In that time I have healed and moved forward. However, there are still those moments when I miss him greatly. This night, the night of the dream, was one of those times. When I climbed into bed that evening, I could not help but wish he were still there in his usual place so that I could slide over next to him and feel his arms around me just once more. And then, shortly after I fell asleep, the dream came.

My dream that night was comforting, but at the same time disturbing. In the dream I had been able to see Ty and be near him, but why could he not put his arms around me and hold me? That detail haunted me. I could not forget how he looked, how he held his arms—outstretched, stiff and straight—refusing to touch me. And the look in his eyes—of sadness, of sorrow—was unforgettable. Yet, buried in the sadness, deep in his eyes, I could also see his love. And I wondered: *Why this dream? Why did it seem so significant?*

The dream could be called a snapshot of the past few years of my life. It stayed with me, and as time passed I began to realize the obvious truths the dream portrayed. Subconsciously, just as in the dream, I have looked for Ty everywhere. Not actually expecting to see him, of course, but no matter where I have gone, no matter where I have been, he has always been in my thoughts and my memories, reminding me of how it used to be—and of how I wish it still could be. So often have I longed to feel his arms around me just once more, holding me close. My dream that night definitely portrayed those feelings. At the same time, the two scenes in the dream in which he held his arms out to the side, stiff and straight, symbolized the fact that this could not happen. My dream helped me accept this reality, and I believe God allowed this experience not only to comfort me but also to strengthen my healing.

Accepting reality is a basic step in the healing process for those who grieve. For me, this meant accepting the fact that I was now truly alone, that a vast void now existed between my husband and me. It meant accepting the fact that I could be close to my husband in my memories, my dreams, my thoughts, my visits to places we had been together, but he could not return to me. This was now my reality. A reality created and shaped by that dreaded enemy of us all: death.

Death enters our lives and forces us into a deep, dark valley, the valley of grief. For a number of years now, that is where I had been.

In the valley of grief.

Reflection

The author feels God was reaching out to her through her dream, offering comfort and strength as she struggled with the pain and loneliness she experienced after her husband's death. God reaches out to us in various ways. How has God reached out to you?

Has there been something that has happened—a dream, something someone said, or possibly something you have read—that touched you in a special way?

How did the incident make you feel?

GRIEF

What is grief? I can only attempt to define it. The dictionary describes grief as intense emotional suffering caused by trouble, remorse, or loss, such as the loss of a loved one. Others describe grief as deep sorrow or mental anguish; others say grief is the process of working through a loss. It is all of that, but, as I have learned, it is much, much more.

Some say that grief is a journey, and I feel this is a good description. It fits. The grieving process is a journey through life which can last a few months, a year, or several years. We each handle grief in our own way, and this may mean that it takes longer for some to heal than for others. Some seem to want to get the whole painful process behind them as quickly as possible, hoping, I suppose, to make their journey shorter. Such individuals, trying to avoid the pain, may hurry to put away everything that reminds them of their loss, such as photos of the deceased, or their loved one's clothing, or other items that belonged to that person. On the other hand, others may cling to memories of their loved one, not wanting to make any changes in circumstances or surroundings.

It was the latter group to which I belonged. I wanted things to stay just as they had always been. I wanted nothing to change. I did not want to move the items on my husband's desk or touch the clothes in his closet. In fact, I brought home the clothes he wore on his final trip to the hospital—a russet-colored shirt and gray slacks—and hung them on the outside of the closet door in our bedroom where I could see them every day. And for two years they stayed there. It took that long before I could bear to move them. I suppose this was my way of trying to keep him close. And it was comforting to see his clothes hanging there, as though waiting for him to take them down and put them on—but, of course, this could never happen. He was gone, and even though this cold, hard fact was embedded in my head, my heart held onto its foolish longing. Feelings such as these, I have learned, are normal, even common among those who are grieving.

It is feelings, or emotions, such as the above that make up the luggage we carry with us on our journey of grief. Usually when we set out on a journey we bring along extra clothing, shoes, a toothbrush and toothpaste, possibly an alarm clock, and other personal items. However, on our journey of grief the luggage we carry is filled with pain, despair, sorrow, loneliness, remorse, unhappiness, sadness, uncertainty, and on and on—all of those painful emotions that grief evokes. There are many emotions involved in grieving, and just as the healing process varies with each individual, the emotions we feel differ from person to person. There is no set scale for measuring, and everyone is different. We each have our own DNA, that special identifier of who we are, and we each handle grief in our own way, that grief relative to:

our understanding of life and death;

our own particular situation;

our individual personality;

and our relationship with the one who passed away.

It is understandable, therefore, that the emotions felt by each person who mourns the death of a loved one could be different and distinct. Nevertheless, emotions are powerful . . . they can stir us into anger, drag us down into depression, lift our spirits in joy. Our emotions affect us in a variety of ways and play a powerful role in the journey of grief.

Grief is something I believe cannot be fully understood—what it is, how it feels, what it does to you—unless or until you have taken the journey. I and countless others, since time began, have walked this road. Perhaps the best way for me to define grief, then, is to tell my story, my journey through the valley of grief, and how, with the Lord's help, I have made it this far—toward healing and wholeness.

Reflection

If you are struggling with grief, list the emotions you have been feeling: i.e., anger, guilt, loneliness, depression, confusion, sadness, despondency, or whatever fits in this space for you.

Which has been the most difficult? Why?

PART II

THE BEGINNING

Set me as a seal upon thine heart,
as a seal upon thine arm:
for love is strong as death . . .

SONG OF SOLOMON 8:6 (KJV)

HOW IT ALL BEGAN

It was below-freezing cold. The kind of cold one would expect on a wintry evening in late January in the Kentucky mountains. The year was 1954, my third year as a student at Berea College, a small liberal arts college in the town of Berea. Mid-semester break was almost over and second semester classes were about to begin. I was in my dorm room preparing for bed when the hall monitor knocked on my door to tell me I was wanted on the telephone. (There were no cell phones in those days, and we were not allowed to have telephones in our rooms.)

Who could be calling me this evening? I hurried out of my room and down the long hallway.

"Hello."

"Hello. Mary Emma?" The voice speaking my name was masculine, strong and clear.

"Yes, this is she."

"This is Claude Tisinger, over in Howard Hall. You probably don't know who I am."

Tisinger . . . hmm . . . Oh, he's the guy who dated Gerry when we were freshmen.

"Well, yes, I do know who you are. How are you?"

"I'm good. I was wondering if you would like to go with me to the junior/senior social Saturday night."

Brief glimpses of a tall, slim, dark-haired, good-looking guy with a ready smile flashed through my mind. I had seen him riding around campus on an English bicycle at times, and noticed him when he was with Gerry (short for Geraldine), of course. But I was going to the social with Gordon.

"Oh, gosh. I'm sorry, but I already have a date."

"Oh . . . " There was a brief pause on the other end of the line. "Well then, how about the next Saturday?" When I didn't answer immediately, he was quick to add: "We could go to the movie in the chapel." The chapel was actually a huge auditorium where all the college's gatherings were held.

Needless to say, I was impressed with his persistence. And Gerry had said he was a really nice guy . . . and I couldn't think of any reason to say no. "Okay . . . yes. I would like that. What time?"

* * *

That's how it all began. Claude was at the social on Saturday evening, alone; I was with Gordon. The social, or party, was sponsored by the college and held in the school's gymnasium. It was a time for juniors and seniors at the school to get together for a little fun and relaxation before buckling down to classes, which were scheduled to begin the next week. Cookies and fruit punch were served (alcoholic beverages were not allowed on campus), and there were a few games for intermingling. As could be expected, Claude and I were very much aware of each other, but he respectfully kept his distance.

When that next Saturday rolled around, Claude arrived a few minutes early at Fairchild Hall, the huge, old Victorian building that served as one of the girls' dorms on campus and had been my home for more than a year. He looked quite handsome dressed in gray tweed slacks and a burgundy vee-neck sweater over a white dress shirt. I do not remember anything about the movie, not even the title—which shows how impressive that story was! After the movie we had coffee in a little restaurant around the corner, a favorite hangout for students, especially in the evenings and on weekends. The restaurant was small and homey, a place where students could relax and get away from studies for an hour or so. And it was there that Claude and I got to know each other better, and where he asked that I call him Ty rather than Claude.

* * *

"Well, Claude," I ventured as we settled into a booth in the noisy, crowded restaurant. "Where are you from?"

He smiled. "My home is in the beautiful rolling hills of the Shenandoah Valley in Virginia. How about you?"

Before I could answer, he quickly added, "And hey, how about calling me Ty? All my friends call me Ty."

"Okay, I like that. Ty it is. You asked where I'm from. My home is in North Carolina. I live just off Route 70, the main highway that runs between Morganton and Valdese—two small North Carolina towns. I live about halfway between. Tell me about your family. Brothers and sisters?"

"Oh yes," he said. There was that engaging smile again as he reached for his wallet to pull out some pictures. "There are six of us, four boys and two girls—and I'm the oldest. There was a little sister, Madeline, before me, but she only lived about two months. My brother Jim is next; then Donald, whom we all call Buck, then Nancy. Nancy is graduating from high school this year. And then there's my youngest brother, Marion, who is fourteen, and my little sister Doris. Doris is ten." Ty had photos of everyone except the little sister who had died.

"There's about two years' difference in our ages," he continued, "until my little sister Doris came along. There's a span of four years between Marion and Doris. And, of course, I have to add my grandmother, Grandma Dellinger. Her name is Gertrude, but everybody calls her Gertie. She lives just up the road from our house, and she comes down just about every day.

"My dad's a mechanic. He works for the Virginia State Highway Department. And my mom . . . she raises chickens to sell and picks apples in the apple orchards in the fall to earn extra money for the family.

"Now it's your turn. Tell me about your family."

"Oh, well." I toyed with my silverware. I didn't like to talk about my family. My mother and father were having problems, and they separated when I left for college. "There's not much to tell. As I said, I'm from Morganton. Morganton is a small town located about halfway between Charlotte and Asheville. You've probably heard of Charlotte and Asheville . . . the *B-I-G* cities. Actually, my address is Morganton, but I live a few miles outside of town.

"I have an older brother, L.A. His name is Leon, but we call him L.A. The A is for Alexander, his middle name. He's currently serving in the United States Air Force, stationed in England. And I have a younger sister, Phyllis, at home. But I also have two older sisters—stepsisters, actually—and an older stepbrother, all of whom are married and have homes and families of their own. They were my mother's first family before she married my father. My father is a carpenter, and my mother works in a cotton mill. She's been working there—in the same place—from the time my brother and sister and I were all in school until now."

As Ty was going through his family, I noticed right away how proud he was of his home and his state, and how close-knit his family was. There were similarities (and differences) in our backgrounds, but it was obvious that both of our families struggled financially.

I was in my third year at Berea at the time, and Ty had just returned to campus after completing two years in the United States Air Force. This was during the Korean War, a time when young male college students were not exempt from being drafted into the armed services. As we talked I learned that Ty received his draft notice at some point during his third year at Berea. He was classified as a junior then, with only one year remaining before graduating with a degree in agriculture. Upon receiving his draft notice, he immediately joined the United States Air Force. Now, having completed his tour of duty, he had returned to Berea to finish his studies and graduate.

I was quite impressed and liked him right away. He had the carriage of an officer and (to borrow the title of a popular

Richard Gere movie) a gentleman. He was handsome, intelligent, charming, well-mannered, and well-liked among his peers. And ... he seemed to like me. That first date led to a second date, then a third, and then many more after that. Before long we were a steady couple . . . walking to class together, meeting for meals in the boarding hall, studying together in the library, dating on weekends. And then, one evening . . .

It was one of those warm, early spring, peppermint-sweet evenings in April, just before spring break. And it was the night the direction of our future was determined. It was a Saturday night and we were outside Fairchild Hall, my dorm. We had been to the coffee shop over on the street for ice cream, or perhaps a Coke, I don't remember which. But some things you don't forget.

Ty put his arm around me, leaned close, and said, "See that moon up there in the sky? If I could, I would reach up, take hold of that moon, bring it down, and give it to you. I can't give you the moon, but this I can do . . . Mary Emma Childers, will you marry me?"

My yes was obvious.

When Ty returned to campus after spring break, he brought with him a diamond ring for my finger—and a big chocolate bunny. (Spring break was wrapped around the Easter celebration that year, and Ty had discovered my yen for chocolate.) The chocolate made its way to my heart, the diamond ring sparkled on my finger, and the sweetness that comes with spring after a long cold winter enveloped us. We made our plans. We would be married in September, return to Berea, I would complete my senior year, and Ty would do a year of post-graduate study.

In the meantime, when the academic year ended in late May, I went home to North Carolina and Ty headed north to Illinois. He had a job lined up for the summer months in Mendota, Illinois, with the California Packing Corporation harvesting peas and beans. Jack, his roommate at Berea, and a number of other friends from the college had been hired also. This was something the guys did each summer, but it was a new adventure for Ty. He and Jack traveled together to the plant where they would harvest crops for market. They were aware the job meant a lot of heavy work in the hot summer sun, but it would provide an income.

While there, Ty wrote often, even before he reached Mendota . . .

Louisville, KY
June 13, 10:00 P.M.

Hi Sweet,

The farther away I get, the tired-er I get, and the tired-er I get . . . Sure wish I were back in North Carolina with you. We left Jack's at 8:00 this morning, and have just about been doing sixty ever since. I feel like 60.

Jack and I just about had our appetites ruined for the duration this morning. We stopped at a place for some tomato juice . . . and they charged us 51 cents for two glasses. We're sort of against tomato juice now.

I forgot to tell you last night, but just before I got to Jack's house . . . my gas tank went dry . . . exactly 15 feet from a gas pump. The man had to use a bucket so I could pull up to the pump. When I thought of all the times you were with me and I never ran out of gas . . . I couldn't help but laugh. For sure it was a poetic injustice.

The miles are awfully long . . . but it helps to think that every one is one less to travel until I see you again. I think sometimes my head should be examined for ever going away and leaving you, but I would never feel right if I couldn't give you some of the things I feel you should have.

Days are long . . . and the evenings lonely, my love . . . I think of you . . .miss you . . . and love you . . . very much.

Ty

Mendota, Illinois

6-14-54, 8:30 P.M.

Hi Sweetheart,

"Here," but there is no enchantment in it . . . Just a lad who is a long way from the girl I sure do love.

We got here about 30 minutes ago and they're sending me out on some camp tonight. Jack will probably be assigned out to-night, or tomorrow. We had an uneventful trip from Louisville, although we did see a wreck about five minutes after it hap-pened. Some people hurt, but nobody killed.

Guess I'm mighty tired right now, but at the immediate pres-ent I don't care if I make no more money than enough to get back to N.C. on. It appears that I'll make a little more than that.

. . . Sure do miss you . . . Wish I had a few moments with you that I could stretch into the hours that were all too short when we were together.

I love you . . . very much . . . and miss you the same amount.
xxx Ty

Mendota, Ill.
Tues., 5:00 P.M.

Hiya Sweet,

We didn't work this afternoon, and with little to do 'cept sleep, I thought I might break the rule and write twice today. Remember that—if I happen to skip a day sometime. . . .

Breakfast and lunch were very good . . . everything that is fattening.

I can't wait to work so's I can eat more. Weighed in Louisville where we stayed overnight. Stripped, I weighed 135, but hope to add as food intake progresses.

The moon up here is just like everything else—lousy. Looks like a piece broken off the North Carolina moon, which was in turn broken off — ?? Were you here, I wouldn't have to look at it and I sure wouldn't want to. I'd put these empty and very lonesome arms where they would rather be than anywhere else and . . . very gently close them about you. The skies would never be as lovely as the blue in your eyes. . . . and . . . each little breeze could tell you how much I care . . . for you . . . They could ask me and I'd tell you . . .

I love you.

Ty

And then, his last letter from Mendota . . .

Mendota, Illinois
July 6, 8:30 A.M.

Hi Sweet,

Without a shadow of doubt, I'm 1/3 Hank Snow . . . always "moving on." Believe me, it gets awfully tiresome and lonely. I've eight hours to spend today before getting paid. The minute that happens, twenty-two hours and 750 miles later, your guy hopes to be home. Wish it was your home, but I'll try to be there one weekend before long . . . I've only one road I wish to travel—and that's the one on the way back to you. Miss you, and love you?? . . . I . . . sure . . . do.

Nobody is working today and possibly not tomorrow. They were supposed to pull weeds from beans today, but there was a storm last night. There were three tornadoes yesterday in Wisconsin—and that's not far from here. Guess we got the tail end. Trees and wires came down everywhere, and I couldn't leave Station 7 this morning until they moved the top of a tree from the road. It was splintered by lightning. Before the rain came last night, the wind really shook that shack I was living in . . . the screen door on each end just banged back and forth. It isn't very often that I get scared, but had you been here, I would most surely have been holding on to you. One could almost read a newspaper by the lightning flashes that came and went with monotonous regularity. Sounds sort of trite, doesn't it? But it was only very real. I was watching it, and thinking of you when I fell asleep . . .

. . . Guess I'll clean up this afternoon and putter around with the car. You'll be getting more postcards, this time from Indianapolis, Dayton, etc. . . .

I love you . . .

         Always, Ty

Ty returned home to the Shenandoah Valley and worked for the Virginia State Highway Department until the middle of August.

A few days later he headed for North Carolina, and on a beautiful September Saturday afternoon (September 4, 1954), in my home church, Pleasant View Baptist, we were married. It was the simplest of weddings. Kathy, my best friend and roommate from college, was my maid of honor, and Ty's brother Donald (Buck) was his best man. Eva, a close friend and my next door neighbor, sang "I Love You Truly," and my pastor officiated the service. The Reverend Carl Hemphill had been my pastor for most of my life. It was he who baptized me when I made that most important of decisions to place my trust in the Lord. On this day he walked me through my vows for another important commitment. A simple wedding—but for both Ty and me it was a lifetime commitment. And a new beginning.

Reflection

With her wedding, the author has just experienced a new beginning. Some beginnings are routine while others are the "big" ones, as the wedding was in her life.

Think of new beginnings in your life. Not just those that are routine, such as the beginning of a new school year, or the start of a new diet, but those "big" ones . . . those really life-changing ones. Changes such as a new job, a move to a new state, things of this nature.

Could you see God's hand at work during those times? If so, how?

NOT TO FORGET

My heart, I gave to you one day,
and gathered yours to mine;
and in that heart you have remained,
untouched by time.

Your smile, your step,
the way you walked
as though the world were yours,
imprinted there . . .
lest I forget.

Your strength became my strength;
your dreams infused in mine.
We faced the night,
and watched the stars break through the dark
and change the gray to light.

Today is ours.
My gift, your gift, is time.
Time to share, the two of us, our love;
more precious still
because we see what lies ahead.

Not to forget . . .
my heart is yours,
and yours is mine.

TOGETHER

After a brief honeymoon in the mountains of North Carolina at a resort called Little Switzerland, we were back in Berea just in time for the beginning of classes, which started the middle of September. We were fortunate to find a small two-room apartment. Actually, it was the entire upstairs of a widow's house in town, the upper floor of which she rented out to students. Our landlady, the widowed Mrs. Potts, was one of those special people the Lord sent across our path, and we got along beautifully with her. She and her husband had purchased this particular house because its location in the small town made it convenient for them, especially since Mr. Potts was disabled.

"I was a few years older than Mr. Potts," she said. "And we always thought I would be the one to go first. But it didn't happen that way. I'm the one who was left behind. We had no children, so now I rent out the upstairs, and I teach piano lessons."

The furnished bedroom, kitchenette, and shared bath were just enough for Ty and for me, and we were close to campus. In truth, it was all we could afford. We were living on the GI Bill, which Ty was entitled to because of his military service. GI, at that time, was a common term for those serving in the United States Army, and the GI Bill of Rights was the name assigned to programs designed by the United States government to help veteran servicemen and servicewomen who served in World War II and since. Benefits of the Bill include education and training at government expense; government-guaranteed loans for homes, farms, and businesses; and job counseling and placement.[1]

I could not contribute anything to our budget. I had not given any thought to attending college when I was a senior in high school because college seemed out of my reach financially. My father's work as a carpenter was sporadic, and my mother was the main wage-earner. She worked in a cotton mill from the time my baby sister started school (and the three of us youngsters were then all in school) until she retired at the age of sixty-two. But I was valedictorian of my class, and my home room teacher, Mrs. Faye Russell, would not let me not go to college.

She suggested I apply to Berea College in Berea, Kentucky. Berea sought students who were highly qualified academically for higher education but from lower-income families (those with an annual income of $5,000 or less). The college did not charge tuition but required that all students work in one of the industries the college sponsored. If it had not been for Berea my schooling likely would have ended with high school and my life would have taken a different direction altogether. In retrospect, I can see now that attending Berea was part of God's plan for me. He was working in my life, opening doors, bringing His plan to fruition.

At the end of that school year, the first nine months of our life together, I graduated with a degree in business administration. Ty held a teaching certificate in biology and science in addition to the degree in agriculture he had received upon graduation the year before. I had originally planned for a teaching certificate in business education, but after learning in February that a baby was on the way, I decided against going that route and changed my major to business administration.

* * *

"I think you're making a mistake," my advisor cautioned.

"Thank you, sir," I said as I gathered up my baby-weighted body and left his office. But I did not change my mind, or my direction.

Have I regretted my decision? As I look back at that time in my life, I remember when the business program (shorthand and typing) became part of the curriculum in my small town high school during my sophomore year, and how I fell in love with the program. I sometimes wonder how our lives might have been different if I had kept to my original plan and gone into teaching. But, at that time in our culture, unless it was absolutely necessary that a mother work outside the home, mothers generally stayed home with their children. Both Ty and I thought it important that this should be our way also— at least until the children were all in school. Yes, I sometimes wonder how things might have been different if I had stayed with my original plan, but I always circle back to reality, and I know that for me—for us—I did the right thing. And now I can see that my love for typing and shorthand—working with words—was the Lord at work in my life. He was preparing me for the writing I do today.

* * *

Should we make our home in North Carolina, near my home? Or in Virginia near Ty's? That was our big question upon graduation. Each of us wanted the other to be happy, so it was an important decision, and we gave it a lot of thought. We talked it over, debated the pros and cons, studied each other's body movements and facial expressions. Finally we decided to settle in the Shenandoah Valley in Virginia, where Ty was born and had grown up, and where he had been offered a teaching position in one of the schools. In September Ty started his first year of teaching and our first child, a blonde-haired, blue-eyed baby girl, was born. Two weeks early, she was born on our first wedding anniversary, Sunday, the fourth of September. We named her Tara.

Four years later, on a beautiful sunny Wednesday in July, in Rockingham Memorial Hospital in Harrisonburg, Virginia, a blond-haired, blue-eyed baby boy joined the family. We named him Darian.

And then, two days before our son turned three, we made a move up the east coast to the flat coastal lands of the state of Delaware to make our home in Dover. This was a big move, and as I look back I see this as another time God opened a door for us. He lifted us out of those beautiful Blue Ridge mountains in Virginia and dropped us down on the shifting sand along the Atlantic shore—where He wanted us to be. His purpose? That remained to be seen.

Reflection

Our Bible tells us that God has a plan for our lives . . . and that He is constantly working in our lives to help us accomplish that plan.

The author now sees her love for typing and shorthand, and working with words, as part of God's plan for her life.

Is there something in your life that you, perhaps, might have seen as coincidental but now realize was the Lord at work in your life?

DELAWARE . . . HO!

Certain events in our lives are so significant they become etched in our memories. I will never forget the day Ty came home from school, walked into the kitchen where I was preparing dinner, moved quietly up, put his arms around my waist, leaned over my shoulder, and said, "How would you like to move to Delaware?"

I turned around, saw the enormous excitement shining in his hazel eyes and the huge smile spreading across his face, and said, "Where . . . *in the world* . . . is Delaware?"

He explained. His high school principal was moving to Delaware to become superintendent of one of the school districts there, and he had promised Ty a teaching position in the high school. We knew very little about Delaware, only that it was a small state on the eastern shore of the United States, and that the Atlantic Ocean was nearby. The clincher for us was that teachers' salaries were higher in Delaware than in Virginia, where we lived. To a family of four struggling to make ends meet, that was magnetic. I am sure Ty knew what my answer would be. Being the romantic that I am, and loving my husband, I would have followed him anywhere.

We made the move on July 27, 1962. How well I remember that last night in Virginia . . .

Our furniture and all our belongings were already on the way to Delaware in the mover's truck, and we were splurging, staying overnight in the exclusive Red Roof Inn in Harrisonburg. I had often stared at that red roof when driving by and wondered about the guests who might be staying there. *Red, the color that often says "Stop! Take care!" So fitting for my mood,* I thought as I lay in bed that night, feeling uneasy, anxious, and wondering, *Are we doing the right thing?* In the morning we would be leaving the beautiful Shenandoah Valley—our home for the last seven years—to drive to Dover, Delaware, and my husband's new higher-paying teaching position. Delaware, the place my mother-in-law labeled "the end of the world."

As I lay in bed thinking about our move to the Eastern Shore, I recalled my first visit to the Shenandoah Valley, seven years earlier. We were newlyweds then, and it was our first Christmas together. Shortly after Ty and I arrived at his parents' home that wintry December evening, there was loud banging on my in-laws' front door.

* * *

"It's the bellsnicklers!" Mom said.

"Bellsnicklers? What's that?" I whispered to my husband as a noisy group of ten or twelve people crowded into the room.

"Just people in the neighborhood—come to visit and say Merry Christmas. It's a local tradition, sorta like Halloween and trick or treat. Without the costumes and the tricks," my

husband explained, as Mom hurried into the kitchen to bring out the Christmas cookies and homemade fudge.

* * *

That was my initiation into the warm, close-knit way of life among the people in the historic Shenandoah Valley, where everyone seemed to know everyone else and there were no secrets. And now we were leaving all of it: the familiar, winding narrow roads; the houses scattered, but more often than not, built near the parents' old home place; the cows and horses grazing on the hillsides; and on warm summer afternoons, the quiet tinkle of a cowbell breaking the stillness.

The next morning as we drove away from the hotel, I looked back a final time.

The red roof glistened in the morning sun, and the Blue Ridge Mountains stood regally in the background. I longed to hold that image, to imprint it indelibly in my mind. We were leaving home, family, everything familiar—and the stately beautiful mountains that surrounded us. I had never known life outside those mountains. And now, like the pioneers of old who shouted "Westward, Ho!" on their trek through unfamiliar territory as they headed west, we were shouting "Delaware, Ho!"

Where . . . in the world . . . is Delaware? Soon, we would know.

Reflection

Has there been a time in your life when you were asked to make a move that you felt would be a life-changing one? Describe that time.

How did you feel? Anxious? Worried about the future? Were you able to find peace about the matter?

In retrospect, how do you feel about the move now?

SETTLING IN

It was about two o'clock in the afternoon when we pulled into the driveway of our new home in Dover. The slate gray ranch-style house we were renting was small, with three small bedrooms, a living room, kitchen, and bath. It was located in Kent Acres, a housing development near the Dover Air Force Base, and it must have been built, at the time, exclusively for the base and its families since all the houses were alike except for the outsides. The exterior slates varied in color. Some of the houses were a dull red, some a dull green, and some slate gray like ours.

Shortly after the moving truck arrived, I sat on one of our suitcases in the empty living room and watched as the movers brought our furniture and other items inside. I was feeling sad and unhappy, wondering, *Will I ever be able to adjust to this new place?*

After the truck pulled away we spent the next couple of hours unpacking a few of our things and then went exploring to find a place for dinner. Minutes later we sat in our car in a huge parking lot at a strip mall with strangers all around us, gray sky above, rain in the air, and an army of seagulls swooping around the car. Listening to the mournful cry of the gulls, I was close to tears, wishing I were back home in Virginia— where there were no seagulls, where the hills rolled up and down instead of the land stretching out in a flat line for miles and miles—where I could feel safe and secure surrounded by the beautiful Blue Ridge Mountains. But we had made our move, and now Dover was home: flatlands, seagulls, and all.

Dover, Delaware's capital city, is a beautiful small town with lots of history, and, as I said, is home to Dover Air Force Base. But, I thought . . . *it is so flat here . . . and smells of the swamp and the sea . . .* The small house we rented was near the Base and we could easily hear the planes revving up, taking off, and coming in, and watch as they flew low over the house. Even so, I liked the fact that we were near the air base, perhaps because it brought out the patriot in me, and it was a daily reminder that we were being protected. But getting used to the military environment, the noise, the flatness, the new and completely different way of life—all this was a big step for someone as adverse to change as I was.

Since it was late July when we made our move to the Eastern Shore, we had a few weeks to settle in before Ty's new job began. After about a month his mother and father came up to see us, and this helped take away a little of my homesickness. Then, shortly afterward, school started and we began to settle into a routine. Ty was excited about his new job, our daughter Tara was enrolled in school, and I was busy with our three-year-old toddler. And we had found a church home in First Baptist Church of Dover.

During Christmas break we were able to drive to North Carolina to visit my family and then on to Virginia to spend a few days with Ty's family. Then, in March, we learned that another baby was on the way. Seven months later a six-pound, five-ounce bundle of Delaware joy—a brown-haired, hazel-eyed baby girl we named Lisa Diane—joined the family.

There's nothing like a new baby to make a place feel like home. Probably because new babies demand so much of your time and keep you constantly busy. Nevertheless, by this time Dover was home for me. Ty was enjoying teaching biology and science in the district high school, and we had been able to obtain a mortgage and purchase our first home in a neighboring development. We moved into the new house in April, about six months before Lisa Diane arrived. The new house was larger, a three-bedroom split-level with a bath and half-bath, and in a great neighborhood. Life was good.

Reflection

Sometimes life seems to move along quietly. During those quiet times when there are no earthshaking or life-changing events occurring around us, and we are busy following our regular routines, we can become "settled in."

Recall times when you have felt "settled in." How did those times make you feel? Happy? Satisfied with life?

Or did you feel perhaps dissatisfied? Wishing for something more? However you felt, describe those times.

PART III

IN SICKNESS AND IN HEALTH

"Lord, the one you love is sick."

JOHN 11:3 (NIV)

LORD, ONE YOU LOVE IS SICK . . .

I loved our new home on Gunning Bedford Drive. It was in a nice neighborhood, within walking distance to a shopping center, close to Caesar Rodney High School where Ty taught, close to our doctor's office, the hospital, shops, and our church in town. And . . . a little farther away from the air base.

We were a traditional family, a young married couple with small children. We struggled with our budget and paying our bills, as most young families do. Especially in the summer months when school was not in session. Those months meant no paycheck for Ty, and since I was not working outside the home, we had to count our pennies, as they say. But we were happy. And life continued along, mostly uneventfully, until that April morning a number of years later when everything changed.

It was 1975 and spring in Dover. This time of year in Dover is almost always a time of beauty. Everywhere, golden yellow forsythia bursts into bloom: jonquils, tulips, and hydrangea seem to pop out of the ground overnight. And the world turns from a wintry gray and brown to a bright springy green. It was an average spring, and we were an average family. Things felt "apple pie-American," just like in a Norman Rockwell painting.

I was a "stay at home mom," and during the twelve years we had been in Dover, Ty had moved from teaching science and biology to serving as science supervisor for the school district. Our three children were all in school. Our youngest daughter, Lisa, was eleven and in sixth grade. Our son Darian was fifteen, a sophomore in high school, and our oldest daughter, Tara, was nineteen and living at home while commuting to classes at Delaware Technical and Community College in Dover. Tara attended the University of Delaware for one year, but then decided to stay home and continue her studies at Delaware Tech.

Several weeks after the beginning of the year, Ty developed a cough that just would not go away. After weeks with no improvement, we finally convinced him to see a doctor, and tests revealed a growth in his throat. After a night in the hospital, and surgery to remove the growth, a biopsy and other tests were performed. The next day as I drove him home from the hospital he was very quiet.

"I didn't have a chance to speak to the doctor this morning," I said. "What does he say?"

Clearing his throat, after a minute or two Ty answered. "The doctor says I have Hodgkin's disease. Have you heard of Hodgkin's?"

Oh no! My heart plummeted. My mind immediately went on silent alert. *Gene, a friend in college, was diagnosed with Hodgkin's shortly after graduation. Gene died about two years later.* Trying to keep my hands steady on the steering wheel, after a moment or two I managed to speak. "Yes, I have heard of Hodgkin's."

"The doctor said I should call and make an appointment to come back and see him about treatment," Ty continued. I could sense the intensity of his words and, with a quick glance, saw the concern in his eyes. But my mind was still grappling with the diagnosis . . . *Hodgkin's!* My friend's face loomed before me and I was filled with fear. *Am I going to lose Ty?* Silence—heavy with anxiety, unspoken questions, and feelings of impending doom—engulfed the two of us for the remainder of the short trip home.

Once at home, hoping to hide my concern, I hurried into the kitchen to begin preparations for lunch. Ty headed for the bedroom, and as soon as he was out of the room I ran to grab an encyclopedia. (Encyclopedias were our resource for information in those days; there was no Internet.) I had to know. What was involved with Hodgkin's? What did this diagnosis mean for us? What lay ahead? I flipped the pages quickly until I found what I was searching for, and immediately I froze, shocked at what I saw. The words on the page burned into my brain:

> *Hodgkin's disease is a serious ailment . . .*
> *The cause is not known, nor is there a cure.*
> *But it is fatal, usually within a few years."*[1]

Fatal! Oh, no! My heart plunged once again, and at that moment my husband walked into the room. He did not hear my silent cry, but he took one look at my face and we fell into each other's arms. And I knew . . . that *he* knew.

We clung to each other, trying to shut out the awful thing that was in the room with us. The threat of death filled the room, billowing around us like a giant shadow, while my normal, secure, and happy little world fell apart. I wanted to offer comfort but I had no source from which to draw; I could only grope for words. Finally, I remembered the doctor's instructions: call and make an appointment to see him and discuss things.

"Ty, we need to call the doctor's office. We need to hear what he has to say."

And then, like a man drowning in the ocean will grab frantically for anything he thinks might save him, my husband grabbed hold of my suggestion—and what we hoped would be a lifeline. A brief phone call followed, and in minutes we had an appointment to see the doctor the following week.

Reflection

Sooner or later, times of crisis come to each of our lives. These may be times of tragedy or times when you receive traumatic news, perhaps concerning life and death.

Perhaps there has been such a crisis in your life. Describe your emotions.

Where do you turn for help in your times of crisis?

A GLIMMER OF HOPE

It was later that night, that April night in the spring of 1975, when I had just learned that my husband had a terrible illness for which there was no cure, that I turned to my Bible seeking hope and comfort. The words from the *World Book Encyclopedia* gnawed away at my insides:

> *Hodgkin's disease is a serious ailment . . .*
> *The cause is not known, nor is there a cure.*
> *But it is fatal, usually within a few years.*

I was consumed with fear, fear that Ty would die. I looked for comfort, for hope, for anything that would take away that awful fear. In prayer I turned to the Lord.

As was my custom I was reading the Bible through, and on this particular night I was reading the Psalms. That night, after everyone was in bed, I sat at the dining room table, my Bible open before me, and read psalm after psalm after psalm seeking comfort and hope. After about an hour I began to notice these words: *You shall yet sing His praise . . .*

They seemed to be popping up over and over. Tired, exhausted, and filled with anxiety, I cried, "God, is this your word for me tonight?"

Of course there was no audible answer. Only silence. I knew in my heart there would be only silence in the room, but I also knew that God speaks to us in other ways . . . one of which is through His Word. *You shall yet sing His praise* . . . These words were words of hope, and I desperately wanted this to be His answer for me. Finally I closed my Bible, and a little later I climbed wearily into bed and eventually fell asleep. All the while, echoing over and over in my head, were those words: *You shall yet sing His praise . . . sing His praise . . . sing His praise.*

Somehow we managed to get through the next few days as we waited to see the doctor. We were eager to see him, but at the same time we were not sure we wanted to hear what he had to say. What if it was not good? We tried to keep alive a small flicker of hope that the doctor's words would be vastly different from what we had discovered in the encyclopedia; somehow we managed to put up a good front for the children. And often, during that time of waiting, I wondered about those words from Scripture: *You shall yet sing His praise . . .*

But I would also say to myself: *Suppose I was mistaken, suppose this was not God's answer to me.* Stubbornly, I clung to my belief—and hope—that it was.

Finally, on Tuesday of the following week, Ty and I sat in the doctor's office and expressed our fears and concerns. I wasted no time; I needed to know if what I had read was true. "Doctor, I read in the encyclopedia that Hodgkin's is fatal, that there is no cure and the patient usually dies within two to three years."

"Well, I don't know what you have read," the doctor replied, "but . . . "—and then he looked directly at Ty as he went on—"we believe we've caught your illness early, and with the proper treatment, we feel you are going to be okay." The doctor proceeded to outline the treatment plan. Ty was to receive cobalt radiation for six to eight weeks for the upper body and then have surgery to remove his spleen. After a few weeks to recover from surgery there would be six to eight more weeks of cobalt radiation, this time to the lower body. The doctor reminded us once again of his belief that the cancer had been discovered early, and he said that, hopefully, with the treatment outlined, the disease should go into remission.

A little later, as we left the doctor's office, Ty reached for my hand. Hands clasped, we walked to our car with a glimmer of hope in our hearts where there had been none.

And within *my* heart, a whisper of gratitude: "Lord, I'm already beginning to sing your praise!"

Reflection

Has there been a time when you searched the Scriptures seeking a special word from the Lord? Describe that time.

What was the answer you received? Was it the answer you had hoped for?

Has this experience strengthened your faith? Why or why not?

THE HEALING

In the 1970s, when my husband's illness was diagnosed, treatment for Hodgkin's lymphoma was not as sophisticated, nor as advanced, as it is today. My husband's treatment, the extensive, full-body cobalt radiation (first for the upper body for six to eight weeks, then for the lower body for the same period), was rough.

First, the treatment was not available at Kent General Hospital, our local hospital in Dover, and Ty had to make a fifty-mile trip north to a hospital in Wilmington, Delaware. His treatments involved about an hour in the hospital (with only a few minutes under the radiation machine) for four or five days each week. The first trip was unforgettable. This was the "discovery" trip—the day the doctors would insert dye into his system to discover how far the lymphoma had spread. The weather was typically April: it was a cool and rainy day. On the trip home we had to pull off the road several times so Ty could step out of the car and throw up; this was thanks to the dye which made him nauseous. Upchucking on the side of a two-lane highway in a cold rain . . . made an already bad day even more miserable.

After that first discovery trip, Ty was able to drive himself to Wilmington for the treatments for a week or so, but then the radiation began to sap his strength. After this, friends in the Caesar Rodney School District office volunteered to drive him the 100-mile-round trip for treatments. He informed his boss and coworkers about his condition and continued with his job, but with reduced hours. We were grateful for the kindness of his coworkers as they worked out a schedule, alternating their days for driving, and, in doing so, took away one of our worries.

Before long Ty began to suffer nausea from the radiation and could not keep food down. He tried. At first he would come to the table for meals and make an attempt to eat, and we all watched in dismay when he would throw up on the spot. It was so bad that the utility bucket I used for cleaning found a permanent spot next to the table. Eventually he gave up trying to keep things normal and stopped dragging himself out of bed to come to the table. Over the weeks his weight dropped from 175 pounds to 125. His strength dropped along with it.

To help him, I tried different foods and different methods of preparing his meals, but nothing seemed to help. Then I discovered that something he *would* eat, and seemed to be able to keep down, were milkshakes. These worked for a while, but eventually he began to refuse those. And then a friend told me about the supplement liquid Boost, a vitamin-enriched drink produced in several different flavors including chocolate, vanilla, and strawberry. Boost became the next nutrient for Ty, and I am convinced that McDonald's milkshakes and Boost helped keep my husband alive.

Often I sat on the bed beside Ty, just to be close to him, when all he could do was simply lie there in his weakness. Often he would say, "I don't know where you get all your energy," referring to all the extra responsibilities that had fallen my way. But that was the least of my concerns. I just wanted him to get better, to recover, to be his old self again. But the future was so uncertain . . .

One morning as I sat by his side, a Scripture I had read earlier in my daily Bible reading popped into my head:

> *Give thanks in all circumstances, for*
> *this is God's will for you in Christ Jesus.*
> 1 Thessalonians 5:18 (NIV)

Frankly, those words were disturbing. *How can I give thanks for this—for Ty being sick like this?* My whole being protested. *I can't. I'm not thankful that this has happened.* But that still, small voice inside of me persisted . . . *Has any good thing come of this? Is there anything you can give thanks for?* My thoughts then went to all who were praying for us. At times it seemed as if we were surrounded by a wall, a wall of prayer, and that wall was protecting us. I knew I was truly thankful for those prayers—and for our friends in church and outside of church who were holding us in prayer. I was thankful, too, that Ty was still alive; thankful for the doctors, nurses, and technicians who were caring for him; thankful for his treatments; thankful that we had hope for his recovery; and I was thankful for the fact that all this made me appreciate and love him even more.

And then I understood. God was blessing us greatly—even in this time of great stress. And I gave thanks.

Reflection

Our Bible tells us that we should give thanks in all circumstances. However, regarding her husband's illness, the author at first found this difficult to do.

Has there been a time—a situation, an event, something that unexpectedly happened—when you felt as the author did? That you just could not be thankful? Describe that time.

Could you, however, give thanks for the good things that came from the situation? Describe those emotions.

How has this affected your faith?

ROBIN WILLIAMS, *DEAD POETS SOCIETY*, AND *CARPE DIEM*

Sandwiched between the two periods of six to eight weeks of radiation treatment, surgery was scheduled to remove Ty's spleen and explore for other cancers. The surgery was performed midsummer. It went well and no other cancer was found, for which we were extremely grateful. After the surgery and a few weeks of recovery, the second phase of the radiation began, and Ty struggled through the remaining six to eight weeks of radiation. By this time he was virtually bed-bound except for trips to the hospital for the radiation treatments.

He seemed able to muster enough strength to make those trips knowing the end was in sight.

And then, in the spring of 1976, one year from the time of the original diagnosis, Ty's Hodgkin's lymphoma was pronounced in remission.

The day we received the good news was a beautiful spring day, bright and sunny. Ty and I were in the doctor's office for his six-week checkup following the end of his treatments.

"Well, Ty," the doctor said, "I have good news for you. You have finished your treatment. And we are happy to say that your Hodgkin's appears to be in remission."

I could not hold back the big smile that began to spread across my face. But my husband, always more cautious than I, immediately asked, "Does this mean that I am cured?"

The doctor paused, rested his chin on his hand, and seemed to give serious thought to his answer. Finally he said, "Let's put it this way. If you can make it through twenty-one years without a recurrence, we will say you are cured."

Twenty-one years! I was ecstatic. At that point in my life, twenty-one years seemed a lifetime. And although Ty never voiced the words, I am sure he felt he had been given a new chance at life. We were both grateful for the healing, the doctors, the nurses and technicians, Ty's coworkers, all of our friends and their prayers, and especially grateful to the Lord. However neither of us, I am sure, realized at the time the prophetic quality of the doctor's words: "twenty-one years." We simply seized the moment. It was a *carpe diem* moment. Thinking back on it reminds me of a favorite movie . . .

Robin Williams, standing tall on top of a student's
desk in the movie Dead Poets Society, *shouting,*
"Carpe diem!" to all the young men surrounding him . . .[2]

Seize the day! It was that kind of moment—exciting, encouraging, wonderful.

We walked from the doctor's office that beautiful spring morning with gladness in our hearts, grateful for healing, glad for life. And with a smile on my face that I could not suppress. Now I could truly sing God's praise.

Reflection

When Jesus walked the earth He healed many. Although He no longer walks among us in human form, the Lord still heals today.

Healing today may be accomplished through doctors and medicines, through surgery, and occasionally we hear of healings that cannot be explained. These healings we tend to call miracles, the touch of God's hand upon us. How have you experienced His healing?

PART IV

THE AFTERMATH

Where can I go from your Spirit?
Where can I flee from your presence?
If I go up to the heavens, you are there;
if I make my bed in the depths,
you are there.

If I rise on the wings of the dawn,
if I settle on the far side of the sea,
even there your hand will guide me,
your right hand will hold me fast.

PSALM 139:7-10 (NIV)

AFTER THE STORM

We all experience storms in our lives—thunderstorms, snow-storms, Northeasters, and possibly even more dangerous and deadly storms such as tornadoes and hurricanes. So we all know or have experienced the aftermath that follows the storm. It has been my experience that immediately after a storm is over there is a wonderful quiet and peacefulness that seems to settle over everything. Maybe that's because all the roar and the fury is over . . . the upheaval, the unpredictability, the anxiety, the worry. All the disturbing elements that accompany storms are behind us once the storm dissipates. The threat of danger is gone; we feel a sort of happiness.

We made it through the storm!

For me, the calm after a storm, the sense of peace and quiet, is like no other. The peace always seems more peaceful; the quiet more quiet than before. But then I notice the debris the storm has left behind and begin to realize: *that debris will have to be dealt with.*

Here in Delaware, Northeasters are fairly common occurrences. When one of these big storms passes through, we can

expect high winds and rain, or sleet and snow, possibly tornadoes. Thus we can all expect, at the very least, to be cleaning
up afterwards. There is plenty of debris—fallen limbs, leaves
blown off trees, trees that have been uprooted or blown over,
damage from flooding, damage to our homes. Nature's storms
can bring damage to our lives in numerous ways—sometimes
minimal, other times catastrophic. This is also true with other
types of storms we face, those difficult trials and troubles that
come our way at various times in our lives, such as what is
termed an incurable disease. And there's always the aftermath.

But God has promised to be with us always. As He was
with me on this Christmas morning a year or so ago . . .

* * *

It was December 25, Christmas morning. I had just gotten
out of bed when my daughter came running in. "Mom, there's
a huge tree down right across our driveway!"

"Oh, no!" We had guests coming. I ran to see. A huge pine
tree had blown over during the Northeaster the night before.
The tree, about thirty years old, was one of several that lined
the long drive extending from our garage to the street in front.
The huge tree had fallen diagonally across the driveway, missing the roof of the house only by inches and blocking access
to the street. We solved the immediate problem by asking our
guests to park their cars on the street, but my daughter and I
were locked in. Since it was Christmas Day, I waited until the
following day to try to find someone to remove the fallen tree.

Early the next morning I began calling. However, I had no
luck.

It was the day after Christmas, and the tree removal companies I had used in the past were not answering their phones. I stopped all calling.

What do I do now? I have to be able to get out of my driveway. I have appointments coming up!

Just then my doorbell rang. I hurried to the door, and there stood a gentleman who, several weeks earlier, had cut down and removed a tree from my neighbor's yard. He asked if he could be of help. I was amazed.

There stood the answer to my prayer—and the timing of his appearance was so perfect. Only the Lord could have arranged it that way. My faith was instantly reaffirmed. Just as He has promised, the Lord is with us, and He provided the help I needed at just the right moment.

* * *

Yes, the Lord is with us in all of life's storms. He is with us not only in the storms of nature but also in those difficult trials and troubles that create havoc in our lives such as struggling with a devastating disease like Hodgkin's lymphoma. And . . . He's with us in the aftermath.

JAPAN 1945

Anyone who has experienced radiation treatment knows that the aftermath, the effects of this particular treatment, can be far-reaching and long-lasting. My first exposure to the word *radiation* came in learning about the drop of the atomic bomb on Hiroshima, Japan, the nuclear weapon that brought World War II to an end in 1945. Called to surrender after the bombing, Japan refused to comply. When a second atomic bomb was dropped on another Japanese city, Nagasaki, a day or so later, Japan surrendered and the war was over.

In Japan, as a result of the bombing, there was devastation for miles and miles, numerous deaths, injuries, and radiation sickness. But it was weeks, months, and years before the full extent of the havoc the radiation caused to the human body was realized, and it became a certain thing that the effects would be long-lasting. Fortunately, over the years we have learned how to lessen the effects of radiation on the human body and still maintain its use for medical purposes.

Radiation helped save my husband's life. Nevertheless, the effects of the radiation on his body were not pleasant. Radiation is a wonderful tool in that it can be a healing agent and destroy unwanted cancer cells in the human body. But, at the same time, it can be quite ravaging as it also destroys healthy cells along with the diseased ones. The disease, Hodgkin's lymphoma, coupled with the radiation treatments, left my husband fifty pounds lighter, not as strong physically, and suffering from depression. But he was alive! And for that we were eternally grateful.

As the weeks and months passed, Ty's health gradually improved. His appetite slowly returned, and with the improvement of his taste and tolerance for food, his weight also improved. Slowly he gained back the pounds Hodgkin's had taken from him, and eventually our lives seemed to be mostly back to normal. However, in looking back, I can see that we never really returned to the "normal" we had before Hodgkin's. The experience brought change into our lives, with the greater change, of course, faced by Ty. And along with the change came a new normal.

For Ty this new period included bouts of depression. We believed the depression stemmed from his illness, from the physical and emotional changes: weight loss, loss of strength, hormonal imbalance, stress, anxiety. In addition, he tired more easily and was more susceptible to colds and other types of minor illnesses. We both believed that the depression would lessen over time and did not feel it necessary to seek professional help. And the depression did lessen as his health improved, and his ready smile came back. Still, there was a difference.

In spite of our joy in his recovery, in his healing, life was not the same. The old cliché, "the honeymoon is over," which has been used so often to describe a change in the relationship between a husband and wife, probably best describes the difference in our lives at this point. It was a subtle difference, but it was there. We both felt it, though neither of us talked about it. It was just that the zest, the excitement, the passion for life that was such a big part of my husband's makeup before the illness seemed to have been burned away by the radiation rays that so effectively destroyed the cancer cells that invaded his body.

And yet, he was alive! And in the aftermath of the storm we had been through, life was our joy.

Reflection

The Scriptures affirm the truth that God has a plan for our lives.

In Psalm 139 we read that each day of our lives, including our last day on earth . . . *all* are written in God's book before we are born.

> *For you created my inmost being;*
> *you knit me together*
> *in my mother's womb. . . .*
> *My frame was not hidden from you*
> *when I was made in the secret place.*
> *When I was woven together*
> *in the depths of the earth,*
> *your eyes saw my unformed body.*
> *All the days ordained for me*
> *were written in your book*
> *before one of them came to be.*
>
> PSALM 139:13, 15, 16 (NIV)

As you reflect on your life, how have you seen God's hand at work?

DEALING WITH THE NEW

During the year immediately following my husband's treatment and recovery, in dealing with this new normal in our lives, it was almost as if we were beginning again. There was a freshness present even though everything was practically the same . . . same house, same daily routines, same responsibilities. And yet we were changed. After all, we had lost an entire year because of his illness. How can you go through a year like the one we had experienced without being changed?

Ty started back to work on a gradual basis. He worked a few hours each day at first, then half a day, gradually working up to full-day status.

During this time a position for a church secretary became available in a nearby church. In view of Ty's illness and the uncertainty about what the future might hold, I applied for the position and was accepted. I love the church, and to work in the church, I believed, would be doing the Lord's work—something I had always wanted to do. Always, while I was growing up, and afterward, I loved being in church, whether it was for Sunday School and worship services on Sunday mornings, Baptist Youth Training Union (BYTU) on Sunday evenings, choir practice and Bible study on Wednesday evenings, or for any of the many reasons there were for me to be in church. I truly loved being there. When I walked through those church doors I felt I was home.

As a young teenager, there were times when I walked into Pleasant View Baptist Church and saw the secretary there, busy at her job, and felt a definite stirring in my heart. I remember thinking, *Now that's something I would like to do.* I did not realize at the time that those stirrings were from the Lord. He placed those longings in my heart to draw me in the direction He wanted me to go. He was guiding my way even then. And now, many years later, when this church secretarial position opened up after Ty's illness—and a need had arisen in our lives—I saw this opportunity as another door the Lord had opened for me. In the Bible, in Proverbs, we read:

Trust in the Lord with all thine heart; and lean not unto thine own understanding. In all thy ways acknowledge him, and he shall direct thy paths (Proverbs 3:5, 6, KJV).

Direct our paths? He truly does.

So now with Ty back at work and me at my new job, and with the children in school, it seemed things were falling into place. However, there were new boundaries in our lives that weren't there before. As I wrote, Ty was not as robust, nor as healthy, and his outlook on life was different. That youthful zest and excitement for life that was his before the illness seemed to have disappeared. And we no longer took life for granted. Nevertheless, he was still with me, living and breathing—I hadn't lost him. We just needed to pick up the pieces and put our lives together again. That was reason to be happy.

Joy, however, does not keep away the shadows. What we experience in life becomes part of us, and the knowledge (or memory) of that experience is tucked away somewhere in the amazing brain the Lord has given each of us. Once stored, research has shown that knowledge (or memory) can stay tucked away, untouched for months or years, or it can resurface at some point, becoming problematic . . . or prove a basis for improvement, for growth. The process is gradual. What happens in the present, *what we are experiencing now, today, pushes what has happened in the past further and further into the background* until it becomes like a shadow—a memory of yesterday. Our experience of that past year—the sickness, the pain, the fears, the threat that the illness could return—all of it, coupled with the physical changes Hodgkin's brought about, was our present reality. And one that could not be easily pushed into the background. So, like a dark shadow, memories of the previous year seemed to be always hanging around in the background, hovering over our everyday lives.

And yet our loving God, in His infinite goodness and mercy, was ever faithful. Just as He is present with us in the storms and difficult disturbances that come our way, He is with us in the aftermath that follows. The Lord sent encouragement—encouragement that came in different forms. At times just a sunny day would be sufficient to brighten our moods; at other times it might be a visit from a friend or friends. Or it might be a card received in the mail, or words from a song. We both were music lovers, and during this time a country music recording called "One Day at a Time" (written by Marilyn Sellars in 1974), rose to the bestseller list. Our friend George gave the recording to us, and it became our theme song. The words were really a prayer, asking the Lord for strength for each day, one day at a time. We listened to the song often, and the words that truly gnawed at our hearts and sent me running for tissues were those about *yesterday*. Those words that said *yesterday's gone . . . and tomorrow may never be mine.* For so long we had been unsure of tomorrow, of what the future held for us. And even now we knew how quickly everything could change and the promise of tomorrow disappear. Quickly we latched onto the hope expressed in the words of the song and made it ours.

Another source of encouragement was our church. I cannot overstate how meaningful our church and church family were throughout Ty's illness and during the years that followed. The church was our bulwark, our hiding place. We were upheld with prayer through the entire year of Ty's treatment, and there were times we were surrounded by a wall, a wall of prayer, and that wall protected us.

And in the church were special friends who took the time to visit us during Ty's illness and afterward. One friend in particular ranks high on the list, John Hill. John was an older man, a salesman, the type of person who never seemed to meet a stranger. John was a deacon in our First Baptist church, and on Sunday mornings he would be the first person everyone would meet when they walked through the doors. John was always there to greet everyone, to learn the names of newcomers and make them feel welcome. During Ty's illness John visited at least once each week. His visits were always brief and cheerful, and Ty and I always felt a little stronger and a little more hopeful after them.

One day, several months after Ty had recovered and the disease was in remission, we thanked John for his kindness in making all those visits.

"John, we just want you to know how much we appreciated your visits when I was sick," Ty said. "You came by almost every week."

"Well, you know," John replied, "there were days when I was tired and I just didn't feel like stopping by to see you, Claude. But . . . I did it anyway."

When John passed away from cancer years later, his absence left a huge void in our church—and in our hearts.

Reflection

God places special people in our lives. Is there a special friend or friends He has placed in your life?

What makes this friend (or friends) special? Why do you feel God placed him or her in your life?

Is there someone to whom you could possibly be a special friend right now?

TWENTY-ONE YEARS . . .
THE GOOD AND THE BAD

"If you survive for twenty-one years without a recurrence of
your Hodgkin's, we will say you are cured."

Twenty-one years. Most would say that covers a large area on the yardstick of life. During those twenty-one years a lot can happen. Both good and bad. The doctor's statement to Ty when he finished his treatment and we learned the disease was in remission established a marker for us. I believe both Ty and I, not openly, but subconsciously, marked off the years as we waited for those twenty-one years—free of illness—to become a reality. It became a sort of unspoken goal to be reached . . . survival for twenty-one years with Ty alive and well.

Why twenty-one? The doctor must have had a reason for that prescribed time frame. We didn't ask why, and he did not explain. Perhaps he considered similar cases to determine how long it might take for the disease to resurface. Nevertheless, no matter how or why the doctor specified twenty-one years, those words marked off a key period in our lives. No matter who we are, what we do, how strong our faith, or what our schedule, life holds both good and bad, and those twenty-one years were no exception. Those twenty-one years the doctor referred to held not only blessings but also their fair share of difficulties, even a few traumas.

The dictionary describes trauma as a severe and painful emotional shock, usually having a lasting effect on the personality. There seems to be no rule as to when or how often traumas can occur. However, as we study the Bible and observe the lives of others, we can see how the Lord uses these difficult experiences and traumas in our lives to strengthen us, to help us to grow, and to enable us to be better equipped to handle the problems that come our way. I do not doubt that Ty's illness with Hodgkin's made us both stronger. And that was a good thing.

ISRAEL

We needed that "greater strength" sooner than we expected. In October, in the year of Ty's recovery from his bout with Hodgkin's, we watched Tara, our oldest daughter, pack her belongings in preparation to heading to Philadelphia to board the Jewish airliner El Al, bound for a kibbutz in Israel. During her year at the University of Delaware, she became interested in the Jewish people and decided she wanted to go to Israel and share the Jewish faith. The year was 1976. Her decision gave us great anxiety and concern; Israel was so far away, and life there seemed so dangerous.

* * *

"Mom, Dad, I'm going to Israel."

"What! What are you talking about?" We were astounded.

"I want to go over there and live . . . and be a part of the Jewish way of life."

"But it's so dangerous over there. How would you live? *Where* would you live?"

"I'll be living on a kibbutz. Arrangements have already been made. I understand I can live and work there, on the kibbutz, for a year. And then I will find a job and move into an apartment. I already have my flight scheduled. I'll be flying over on El Al."

* * *

The day Tara left for Israel was one of those red-letter days in our lives. One you never forget. We said our goodbyes, watched her walk across the lawn (her friend was driving her to the airport), and then watched until their car disappeared from sight at the end of the street. Then I followed Ty into the house and into the bedroom where he had gone to hide his tears. I can count on one hand the times I witnessed my macho husband shed tears—and this was one of those times. We held each other close and cried together, and the emotions we felt—anxiety, worry, fear, sadness—were more intense because the event followed so closely the stress of the year we had just gone through with Hodgkin's. We did not want Tara to go to Israel, but the decision was not ours to make. Our firstborn was now an adult; the decision was hers. Even though we tried, we had not been able to change her mind. We could only offer our support, prayers, and love.

The days immediately following were anxious ones, for there was no word from Tara, and three weeks slipped by.

Israel was not the safest place to be—not then, in 1976, nor now, more than forty-six years later. We were very concerned. Especially in the beginning when there was no mail and we had no telephone calls. Finally, in the fourth week, a letter came; once we knew she was okay, the tension eased.

In Israel Tara lived for a year on a kibbutz and then found an apartment in Tel Aviv.

She worked at the University of Tel Aviv for about a year and then took a position with the Bat D'Or Ballet Dance Academy. She worked at Bat D'Or for the remainder of her time in Israel.

THE GOOD . . . GRADUATIONS, WEDDINGS, AND GRANDSONS

In the meantime, here at home, in addition to our joy in having Hodgkin's and all of the stress and anxiety of that illness behind us, we were experiencing other happy and memorable moments. Darian completed four years of college and graduated from Salisbury State University in Salisbury, Maryland—with wedding bells scheduled to take place a few weeks later. And then, on Saturday, June 6, 1981, in a stately historic hall on the campus of Salisbury State, we welcomed a daughter-in-law, Joan Culver, into the family. It was a beautiful wedding.

During this same time Lisa was graduating from high school. Both Lisa's graduation, and Darian and Joan's wedding, were happy occasions for all of us—and for Tara too, evidently, for she decided to come back to the States for her brother's wedding and sister's graduation. She returned to the U.S. in June 1981 and made the decision not to return to Israel. In the fall she resumed her studies with Delaware Technical and Community College, and after graduation began her career as a legal secretary, eventually earning a paralegal degree. Four years after her return from Israel she served as a bridesmaid in her sister's wedding. Lisa was married in the spring of 1985, a few weeks before her graduation from the University of Delaware. Now our family had grown to include a daughter-in-law and a son-in-law, Travis. In 1995 our first grandson, Anthony, was born. And then, in 1999, we were doubly blessed with the birth of twin grandsons, Ethan and Eli.

Many times during those twenty-one years I recalled the night following the diagnosis of my husband's illness and my desperate plea to the Lord as I searched the Psalms for hope. And many times I recalled the words I was given that night: *You shall yet sing His praise.* I marveled at the awesome wonder of the Almighty God we serve. I marveled at His great love for us, His faithfulness, His very presence with us. We had so much to be thankful for; I could do no less than to sing His praise.

But those twenty-one years also held concerns.

THE NOT SO GOOD . . .

During those twenty-one years—from the end of my husband's treatment in 1976, until 1997—other health problems emerged. A few years after Ty's bout with Hodgkin's, a spot on his jawline began to bleed, and the bleeding persisted. Diagnosed as a squamous cell skin cancer, the cancer was a very aggressive type that kept returning no matter the treatment the doctor used. Finally, a plastic surgeon was consulted and the cancer removed surgically.

However, after four or five years, the cancer was back again, and additional surgery had to be performed. This time a skin graft was necessary to cover the surgical site. And a few years later, at the very end of the twenty-one year period, another trauma awaited us.

In the spring of 1997 Ty was diagnosed with cancer of the bladder. Ironically, this new diagnosis came exactly twenty-one years following our "Robin Williams *carpe diem*" afternoon, the day we sat in the doctor's office and received the great news that Ty's Hodgkin's was in remission. The day Ty asked, "Does this mean that I am cured?" When the doctor answered, "Well, let's say if you can go for twenty-one years without a recurrence, we will say you are cured." It wasn't Hodgkin's this time, but it was cancer—and a cancer that was aggressive.

Surgery was performed to remove the cancer from Ty's bladder. Within six weeks the growth was back, larger than before. Surgery was again performed to remove the growth; once again, within six weeks, the cancer returned, larger than before. Then, a third time, the cancer was removed surgically. Again, within six weeks, it returned.

"It's time to start thinking about removing the bladder," Dr. Kim, our very capable physician and surgeon, advised. "The cancer is now against the wall of the bladder, and there's danger that it can spread to other organs and tissues if not removed."

The fourth surgery, then, was an ostomy. An ostomy involved removal of the entire bladder and rerouting waste from the urinary tract out of the body, through an opening in Ty's side, into a disposable plastic bag worn outside the body.

Needless to say, his life—our lives—once again were completely altered. Eventually, he and I adjusted to the changes that ensued, and we learned how to cope with the physical changes as well as the severe bouts of depression that resulted. It took a while, however; this adjustment happened over time. I believe this experience was more devastating for my husband than the Hodgkin's had been. He had been told he would be able to do all the things he did before—within limits—and I suppose he was able to reach that point: within limits. Eventually we came to a place that seemed comfortable, a place in which we felt our lives were becoming more normal, more satisfactory—only to be faced with a new problem.

AND STILL MORE . . .

It was a Monday morning in August following a very warm weekend. Not long after breakfast I stepped out onto the Florida room where Ty was sitting. "I feel really lousy," he said.

"You look rather lousy," I replied, a bit facetiously. For someone who had been working outside and had just come in from the warm, but not yet hot, Delaware sunshine, he looked pale and anemic. "You have been complaining all weekend of not feeling very well. Why don't we give Dr. Austria a call and ask him to check you over?" I was quite concerned.

Surprisingly, Ty agreed. Usually, he was reluctant to take this step. Dr. Austria immediately made room in his busy schedule to see Ty that afternoon, giving him the last appointment of the day. The doctor discovered that Ty was bleeding internally and sent him straight to the hospital's emergency room for what we thought would be an overnight stay. That stay turned into a three-day one. During those three days Ty was given several platelet transfusions. However, the internal bleeding continued, and at the end of the three days the doctors were still lacking a definite diagnosis as to what had caused the bleeding. It was decided to transfer Ty to Christiana Hospital in northern Delaware for more testing. At the end of the week we had a diagnosis. My husband was suffering from a serious platelet disorder known as idiopathic thrombocytopenia. According to his doctor, this meant his platelets were being destroyed by his immune system just as soon as his bone marrow produced them.

For this newest development Ty was treated with prednisone. Prednisone, I was told, is viewed by many as a "wonder drug," one used to treat many different illnesses, and I believe it did help keep Ty's condition under control. However, like most medicines, prednisone carries side effects which, in the long run, can cause additional problems. One of the side effects was weakening of the bones; another was depression, which, like a friendly relative, kept dropping in and out of our lives. As time passed, these two side effects caused significant problems for Ty. In addition to being depressed, he began to experience pain in his left thigh, and this eventually made it necessary for him to walk with the aid of a walker.

In the midst of all this, by the end of 2007, the cancer on his jawline popped back into the picture. Extensive surgery was again performed to remove the cancer. A section was taken from his chest to create a flap to cover the surgical area on his face; a skin graft, using skin from his upper thigh, was performed to cover the area on his chest. Nevertheless, almost two years later, in November 2009, just before Thanksgiving, we learned that the cancer had dug in even deeper.

It was a cold, windy November afternoon. I stood behind Ty's wheelchair in the doctor's office as we waited for the doctor's summation.

"The surgery," the doctor explained, "would be extensive and would take more of your jaw, and probably part of your jawbone. It would have to be done at Penn in Philadelphia, and would require a team of physicians . . . for an extended period of time. And I'm not so sure . . . " He paused, then continued. " . . . that you would survive the surgery."

It was at this point, I believe, my husband simply gave up.

Reflection

He has showed you, O man, what is good.
And what does the Lord require of you?
To act justly and to love mercy and to walk
humbly with your God.
MICAH 6:8 (NIV)

The will to live is strong. History has shown we will fight to hold onto life, to our last breath.

Sometimes, however, an individual reaches a point where he or she simply gives up, as the author's husband seemed to do. Even though his faith was strong.

Some might see giving up as a sign of weakness, or a lack of faith. On the other hand, could it not show strength, or a strong faith?

A faith that would enable one to "let go" . . . *and to walk humbly with God.*

PART V

THE END OF THE ROAD

*When Jesus saw her weeping, and the Jews
who had come along with her
also weeping, he was deeply moved in spirit
and troubled . . . Jesus wept.*

JOHN 11:33, 35 (NIV)

SILENT NIGHT

It was December 2009. Thanksgiving was over and Christmas was on its way. The neighbors were busy stringing lights along the roofs of their houses and decorating trees on their lawns. For us, though, this year was different. The Christmas tree was up and the decorations were on the tree, but my heart was not into the festivities. During the second week of December Ty was admitted into the hospital once again, and the prognosis was not good.

Each day I drove to the hospital to be with him, and over and over I walked the long corridors to his room soothed by strains of "Silent Night" and other Christmas carols that filtered through the air and drifted slowly down and around the annual display of Christmas trees adorning each floor. Everything was beautiful. I've always loved the Christmas season, and especially the carols, but this year "Silent Night" nicked my heart with pain. For many weeks and months afterward, I could not hear those familiar, beautiful words without bursting into tears. Even now, several years later, the melody dredges up memories of the pain and sadness I felt as I walked those hospital halls with the realization that *my night*, and all the nights thereafter, were truly sliding into silence.

By this time Ty's condition had grown much worse. In addition to the constant pain in his legs, he was dependent upon drugs, unable to walk unaided, and battled a kidney infection as well as congestive heart failure. All of this was exacerbated by the return of the skin cancer on his jawline. The cancer bled continuously.

On Christmas Day, December 25, 2009, Ty and I and the family celebrated Christmas in the hospital. It was a somber celebration. The weather was bitterly cold and a recent snow left icy patches here and there, and these refused to go away. It was Christmas weather . . . truly fit for Santa and his sleigh, with freezing temperatures and ice and snow. But now the icy patches had worked their way from the frozen ground outside the buildings to the inside, forming a chill around my heart.

The family was all there in the hospital room: Tara, our oldest daughter; our son Darian and his wife Joan; and our youngest daughter Lisa with her husband Travis and our three grandsons. (Anthony, the oldest, was fourteen, and the twins, Ethan and Eli, had just celebrated their tenth birthday on December 3.) One of the most touching moments of the afternoon was the moment Ethan, the older of the twins by eight minutes, said, "Granddad, we're praying for you. We miss you, and we want you to get better and come home." Granddad was quiet, but he managed a weak smile.

Normally on Christmas Day all the family would gather in our home for lunch or dinner, and afterward we'd crowd around the Christmas tree to exchange presents. Not this

Christmas. My heart was telling me that our time together—our time with Ty—was growing shorter, but I did not want that to be true. Ever hopeful, I envisioned my husband back home with me. This time, however, it was not to be.

Reflection

God speaks to us in various ways, and one of those is through music. In turn, we can communicate with Him and each other through music.

It is difficult to sing that beautiful hymn, "In the Garden," without feeling God's closeness in a special way, or the soul-stirring "How Great Thou Art" without a heart and voice filled with worship and praise for the Lord.

The beloved carol, "Silent Night," now and forevermore at Christmastime will stir up memories for the author of her husband and their life together.

Are there certain hymns, or songs, that are especially meaningful to you? Why?

LEFT

When the Christmas holiday was over and members of the family were back in their respective homes, at work, or in school, I was running back and forth, in and out of the hospital, wanting to be at Ty's side as much as possible. On Monday, December 28, the day before my husband died, I was at his bedside most of the day. My journal entry for the day:

Monday, December 28, 2009

Oh God,

It's been such a long day and I'm so tired. But I don't want to go home, I'm going to stay here in the hospital tonight. I just want to be with Ty . . .

He was so sweet this morning. After I gave him his shave, I remarked, "Now you look more like that handsome fellow that I married." He reached up, drew my head down and kissed me on the mouth. Tears filled my eyes. I will never forget that kiss, Lord, or the look in his eyes . . . His kisses have been few, and far between, for a long while now.

"I love you, Ty," I whispered.

"I love you, too." His voice was gruff.

An hour or so later, as I sat by his bed holding his hand, his grip tightened suddenly and then loosened. "You squeezed my hand," I said. There was no reply. "That's because you love me, isn't it?"

Again there was a gruff, "Yes."

At lunch time he tried eating for me, but he began to cough and the nurse had him stop. That was when they put the oxygen mask on.

The mask never came off. Ty drew his last breath about twenty-four hours later, at 12:42 PM on Tuesday afternoon, December 29, 2009.

Reflection

Watching the final hours of a loved one's life slipping away is heartbreaking.

The Bible tells us to "so number our days, that we may apply our hearts unto wisdom."

How would you explain the phrase, "apply our hearts unto wisdom"?

THE EMPTINESS

When I walked into our home that Tuesday evening after Ty's death, the emptiness rushed to greet me. As I stepped across the threshold, the realization that Ty would never walk through that door with me again—that we would never again do any of our usual, ordinary activities together—hit me. The pain was agonizing.

"Oh, God," I cried in the silence. "What am I going to do with the rest of my life?"

So many months, months that turned into years, had been spent caring for my husband, meeting his needs. Our biggest concern for almost half of our life together had been his health. My thoughts were a jumble, with memories of the happier times in our fifty-plus years of marriage intermingling with the anguish of more recent events. But now all of that was gone. Everything was different. I was alone—for the first time in my life. And I could not imagine life without my husband.

The house seemed dark, cold, and empty; the darkness was heavy and smothering. I longed to just crawl into bed and pull the covers over my head to shut everything out. However, much later when I turned out the lights and wearily lay down, I found that "everything" crawled right into bed with me. I shut my eyes, but "it" was still there. My husband was gone; he would never be coming back. But the pain that consumed me was not going away.

Reflection

God blesses us in many ways. Great is His faithfulness; it begins anew each morning. Yet we take so much for granted and often forget that things can change . . . and sometimes change quite quickly.

Think about your life. What have you taken for granted?

Think of three blessings you have experienced today, and thank the Lord for those blessings.

SAYING GOODBYE

The days that followed were mechanical ones. All the necessary things that had to be done . . . *had to be done.* Numb, I could only move hour by hour. I felt as though life had lost its meaning. But time doesn't pause when your world is shattered; the earth keeps spinning. God's sun and moon continue their rounds.

Our daughter Lisa, her husband Travis, and our oldest daughter, Tara, went with me to the funeral parlor to make arrangements for the services. Decisions were made on the type of casket, the place, and the time, ever mindful of New Year's Day, which was just ahead. We wanted to choose a time that would allow relatives from North Carolina and Virginia to attend. Finally, the funeral was set for the coming Saturday, the second day of the new year.

Saturday, January 2, 2010, dawned bitterly cold and windy. Temperatures had been hovering around freezing all week, and this day was no different. The children and grandchildren gathered in our home for the trip to the funeral home. Before we left, we all stood in a circle in the family room, joined hands, and had prayer. A short prayer was all I could manage, but it was important that we ask God to be with us, to give us the strength we needed for what lay ahead. And soon we were in the funeral chapel, where friends and relatives gathered for the service.

The Reverend Wilbur Bubb, a former chaplain at Dover Air Force Base, officiated. Ty and I got to know Pastor Bubb when he was interim pastor for First Baptist Church of Dover several years before. The Reverend Roland Coon, lead pastor of Calvary Assembly of God, assisted. During those last few years when Ty was not attending church, I worshiped at Calvary Church, which was close to our home. Feeling that Calvary would most likely play a significant role in my life in the future, it was important to me to have someone from Calvary at the service. Pastor Coon graciously agreed to my request to assist, and he presented the pastoral prayer.

Pastor Bubb began:

We greet you this afternoon in the name of our Lord Jesus Christ.

We have come today to honor and pay our respects to a beloved husband, father, grandfather, brother, and friend . . . Claude Tisinger.

As the service continued—throughout the prayers, the readings, the music (Janet Englehart Schrader sang "His Eye Is on the Sparrow," and "How Great Thou Art," two of Ty's favorite songs), and through Pastor Bubb's message—comfort and hope were extended.

I especially appreciated the reading of the mottoes from plaques Ty kept on the wall above his desk at home. I especially remember this one, by Alan Grant:

I asked God for all things that I might enjoy life.
God gave me life that I might enjoy all things.[1]

I remembered how those words held new meaning for Ty after his battle with Hodgkin's, and how he would quote them at various times. But the words Pastor Bubb read from this plaque (author not given) truly defined the man Ty was.

THAT MAN IS A SUCCESS

who has lived well
laughed often and loved much;

who has gained the respect of intelligent men
and the love of children;

who has filled his niche
and accomplished his task;

who leaves the world better
than he found it,
whether by an improved poppy,
a perfect poem
or a rescued soul;

who never lacked appreciation
of earth's beauty
or failed to express it;

who looked for the best in others
and gave the best he had.[2]

The casket, draped with the United States flag in honor of my husband's service in the Air Force, remained closed throughout the service, for Ty had stated repeatedly that he did not want his casket open when the time came. However, I made a request beforehand that the casket be opened at the end of the service for family members only. This one last glimpse of him, I felt, was important for all of us—especially for me. And as family members gathered around the casket to say that last goodbye, my sister Phyllis wrapped her arms around me and I wept on her shoulder. Ty's brothers, Jim and Buck, who had driven up from Virginia, and others wept also. In retrospect, I've never regretted the decision to open the casket, even though it meant going against my husband's wishes.

Reflection

When someone we love dies, there are many things to be taken care of, including planning the funeral or memorial service, meeting burial requirements, and notifying relatives and friends . . . all while trying to deal with grief.

The author was torn between honoring her husband's wishes that his casket not be opened at the service and her feeling that it was important, not only for herself but also for other family members, to be able to have that final glimpse of him.

Recently a friend of the author passed away. The friend had previously stated that she did not want a funeral or memorial service for herself when the time came.

Would you honor such a request from someone you loved?

THE FINAL STEP

The Lord is close to the brokenhearted and saves those who are crushed in spirit (Psalm 34:18, NIV).

The interment followed. The procession to the cemetery moved slowly, as it should have, for we did not want to hurry. It was a trip like no other, and my feelings were difficult to describe. I felt cold, abandoned, alone. I felt that everything light and warm and happy had gone from my life. And, all the while, my heart was filled with dread at what was to come, the final step of my husband's life: the interment.

Once we reached the cemetery, I stepped through the frozen muddied terrain to stand by the casket; now the word "alone" took on new meaning. Surrounded by friends and family, I had never before felt so alone as I did in those moments—as I stood before the cold metal box in which lay the lifeless body of the man with whom I had spent most of my life. The man with whom I had built a life. It was the lifeless body of the man with whom I had borne three children and watched them grow into adults. The lifeless body of the man with whom I shared the joy of the birth of our three grandsons, and together we watched them grow. And now that body was going to be lowered into the ground, and the ground shoveled over him from above, hiding completely any evidence of his presence. That was finality—the bitter, cold, windswept face of *my* reality.

The pastor presented a short message, followed by a prayer, as we gathered around the casket, and then it was over. As I stood there in the bitter cold, I was comforted in the remembrance of Scriptures, and the words of our Lord when He said to his disciples (and to all who believe in Him):

> *In my Father's house are many mansions:*
> *if it were not so, I would have told you. I go to prepare*
> *a place for you. And if I go and prepare a place for you,*
> *I will come again, and receive you unto myself;*
> *that where I am, there ye may be also (John 14:2, 3, KJV).*

The Lord was with us in the cemetery that cold January afternoon, and I clung to Jesus' words. They were my comfort and hope—my hope that someday I would be able to see Ty and be with him again.

The Lord was there. Always His love surrounds us. And I know that He cares.

Reflection

UNTIL TOMORROW

God gave us yesterday.
He willed our lives to touch,
to love, to laugh, to dream,
to share both joy and sorrow.
And then, He called you home.

Today I stood beside your grave;
a lonely place,
for sad and broken hearts,
with only the wind to hear
when I called your name.

I like to think you heard,
desiring, oh, so much,
once again to have you near;
and then, God whispered,
"Tomorrow."

So now, when the world is still,
and my lonely heart is filled
with remembering;
amid the shadows and the tears,
God's promise echoes clear . . .

joy will erase the pain,
and we will touch again,
in His presence,
in His time,
in His tomorrow.

NIGHTFALL

After the funeral services, following the interment, everyone was invited to the local Roma restaurant to share a meal. I noted the number of friends and family who filled the room in the Italian restaurant, and it was comforting to feel their support. However, as should be expected, the atmosphere was subdued, and underneath it all I felt a terrible sadness and sense of despair, and I had no appetite for food. A few hours later the long, difficult day was finally over, and except for immediate family, friends and relatives said their goodbyes as we left the restaurant. Tara planned to stay with me for a few days, but the rest of the family left shortly afterward for their homes.

The house now seemed even more cold and empty, the darkness that surrounded me even darker. Knowing that Ty was gone, that I could not see, nor touch, nor speak to him again created a dreadful void. Those days surrounding my husband's death were the darkest of my life. Death takes us to a place where no one ever wants to be, but . . . we have no choice once death takes us there.

Dealing with the reality that our loved one is truly gone is one of the first, and most difficult, of the problems we must face. Yet this is also one of the first requirements toward healing. We have to accept the fact that the one we loved is no longer here—and we must begin to cope with his or her absence. The pain and anguish is so severe at first that it seems we can only strive to survive—to get from one moment to the next, from one hour to the next, from one day to the next. It is only as time passes and we are forced to deal with the absence of that loved one on a daily basis, forced to deal with all of those emotions our grief forces upon us, that reality begins to sink in.

And finally the truth takes root and the fact becomes real. Our mind may tell us what is true, but it likely takes a while for our heart to accept that truth, to catch up.

Reflection

There is a popular saying: *Time heals all wounds.* How do you feel about this statement?

In describing the death of her husband, the author shares some of the most painful moments of her life—and the difficult task of having to accept the reality of death.

The author's strength came from her faith and trust in the Lord. Where do you find strength to face life's most difficult situations?

PART VI

ADJUSTMENT

I waited patiently for the Lord;
he turned to me and heard my cry.
He lifted me out of the slimy pit,
out of the mud and mire;
he set my feet on a rock
and gave me a firm place to stand.
He put a new song in my mouth,
a hymn of praise to our God.
Many will see and fear
and put their trust in the Lord.

PSALM 40:1-3 (NIV)

THE DAY AFTER

The day after. How often we celebrate certain days in our lives: birthdays, graduations, anniversaries, Christmas, New Year's Day, Valentine's Day, Thanksgiving Day, Easter, the Fourth of July—the list goes on. But how often do we think about, remember (or even want to remember), the day *after* a significant event?

Sunday, January 3, 2010 was the day after my husband's funeral. The day after I said goodbye to Ty for the last time. The day after I stood beside his casket, knowing it was to be lowered into the ground, then covered with heaps of dirt, to be hidden forever. It was the day after the end of my life, it seemed.

On this day after Tara was with me. She would be leaving in a couple of days, returning to her apartment in Wilmington. Neither of us had much to say for the entire day. It was another bitter, cold, wintry January Sunday. The house was warm, yet in the emptiness that filled the house, our hearts were cold.

And I had a decision to make. I was president of The Dover Century Club, a volunteer women's club, and our executive board was scheduled to meet the following morning. What should I do? I did not want to go into town, open the clubhouse, and conduct a meeting. I just wanted to curl up on the couch and be left alone. But there wasn't time to cancel the meeting, and even if that were possible, sooner or later the meeting would have to take place. My other option was to have someone else take charge, but I still would have to talk to that person and relay all the essential information she would need. And *that* . . . I did not want to do. On the other hand, what would I do if I sat at home and decided to postpone the meeting? *You will just sit at home and cry* . . . my inner voice prompted.

So on Monday morning, the day after the day after, I went to town, opened the clubhouse, and we had our board meeting.

The obituary had been published in *The Delaware State News*, our local newspaper, and several of the ladies in the club had attended the funeral services. So word of my husband's death *had* gotten out. On Monday morning I could see that some of the club members were surprised to see me when they arrived for the meeting. But no one voiced the words.

"Ladies," I began, "I had a choice. I could have sat at home this morning and . . . " I choked on the words. " . . . and cried. Or I could come in, and we could have our meeting. I decided not to sit at home and cry. Thank you for coming. I call the meeting to order."

The ladies were considerate and sympathetic. They moved quietly around me, and everything went smoothly. By noon the meeting was over and soon I was back home—back among all the reminders of what I had lost.

THE "TO DO" LIST

The funeral home director had given me a list of important actions that needed to be taken care of before the funeral, and a longer list to do after the funeral. We discussed the "before" items when we had our meeting with the director to plan the services. These included: ordering the flowers (if not taken care of by the funeral director); making arrangements for clothes to be taken to the funeral home, along with other pertinent items such as eyeglasses, jewelry, and a recent photograph of the deceased; and selecting photos for the slide show that would be shown during the service.

The "after" list was much longer and was basically the same as other lists I had received from other sources. The listing contained items I would need to take care of, including:

1. Obtain copies of the death certificate from the funeral director.

2. If necessary, consult a lawyer (estate/probate).

3. Locate important papers (safe deposit box).

4. Contact agent or life insurance company.

5. Contact the Social Security office.

6. Contact Ty's employer (in this case, the pension office).

7. Contact the bank.

8. Contact the Register of Wills, probate court, and file the will.

9. Contact the Division of Motor Vehicles if a vehicle title needs changed.[1]

Such a long list! It was overwhelming. *How will I ever be able to get all of this done?*

Nevertheless, all of it needed to be taken care of. And so, when Tara suggested we go to the bank and take care of all the changes that needed to be made there, I called and set up an appointment for the next day. I also called the funeral home to see about the death certificate and was told I could pick it up the next day also.

At the bank the following day, Tara waited in the lobby while I met with Lori, the financial consultant. No one could have been more thoughtful and kind as we went over the accounts to see what needed to be done; even so, it was painful. In a manner of speaking, each time we erased Ty's name from an account, it was like losing him all over again.

About two hours later we were finished in the bank and back in the car. "Mom, why don't we go over now to the Register of Wills' office?" Tara suggested.

Leaning my head against the steering wheel, I cried, "I can't! I can't do any more today." I knew Tara would be leaving soon, going back to her apartment in Wilmington, and I realized she was only trying to help with all the loose ends that needed to be tied up before she left.

But at that moment I could not do any more. Those two hours in the bank, removing Ty from our accounts, left me emotionally drained. But I had also learned from Lori that there were certain steps that could not be taken with our bank accounts until the will had been registered, so when we reached home, I called the Register of Wills office and made an appointment for the following day.

Tara left early the next morning to return to her Wilmington home, and I was alone again. At two o'clock that afternoon, I entered the Register of Wills office with a copy of the death certificate and our will in hand. There too, as in the bank, I was treated with kindness as I filled out the necessary forms and registered the will. At one point the Registrar came over to speak to me. He said only four words, but it was his facial expression and the manner in which he spoke that gave me comfort. His words: "It's hard, isn't it?"

I could only nod my head and whisper "yes" as the tears I had been able to hold back until then began to well up in my eyes.

It's hard, isn't it? His words—just four simple words— showed an understanding of the pain I was experiencing, and they meant so much to me. I could see kindness and understanding in his eyes; I could hear it in the tone of his voice. I could also see that he too had walked the road of grief, that he understood how I felt. Once you have walked this road, it's easier to identify others who have done so. The pain of grief is hard to hide.

* * *

Two years had gone by since my husband's death, and I was attending the Greater Philadelphia Christian Writer's Conference near Philadelphia.

"I can always tell," the workshop instructor said, looking directly at me. He was discussing writing, and our emotions, and was referring to individuals who were going through a period of depression, sadness, unhappiness, or grief. "I see it in their eyes."

I totally agree—our eyes give away our secrets.

* * *

MASKS . . .

During the days and weeks following the funeral, as I walked the road of grief in this new world I had been forced into, I found that knowing what to say and how to comfort those who have lost a loved one is sometimes problematic. It may be difficult to find the right words to say, and we certainly don't want to say the wrong thing. I have also learned, from my experience, that we do not know, or cannot know, what the other person (that individual we meet on the street, or in the store, or wherever we may be) is experiencing.

* * *

I was at the checkout counter in the local grocery store. It was the third of July, approximately six months following Ty's death.

The lady on the other side of the counter looked tired.

"Are you working tomorrow?" I asked. "It's the Fourth of July."

"Oh, yes," she stoically replied, with deadened eyes that looked as though they would never smile again. Then she continued. "I just lost my husband." She paused. "And in fact, I'm working two jobs. When I leave here, I go to my second job."

In silence, I shared her suffering.

* * *

We all wear masks. In passing others on the street, in walking up and down the aisles in the grocery store, or sitting in the pew in church, this fact has become clear to me. I cannot know what is going on in the life of the stranger sitting next to me in church, or in the life of the person standing behind the checkout counter in the grocery store . . . any more than he or she can know that I am grieving the loss of my husband. However, I have also observed that when others know you are grieving, they usually do want to be of help and offer sympathy. And showing that they care can be as simple as acknowledging that they know you are hurting—by giving you a hug, or through simply saying, "How are you doing?" Or, perhaps, "It's hard, isn't it?"

Our twin grandsons Ethan and Eli had just turned ten, three and a half weeks before their grandfather passed away. A few weeks after the funeral, I was staying overnight with them. At one point Ethan approached me. "Mom-Mom," he said. "When you feel sad, think of something happy."

I was touched. "Thank you, Ethan," I replied as my eyes grew moist. "I will try to remember to do that." And even though my supply of happy things to think about at that time was rather low, I knew Ethan said those words out of love for me, and that made all the difference.

Reflection

In the Bible (Job 2:11-13), when Job was grieving, his close friends (there were three) came to him and, for a while, simply sat with him. They were offering their sympathy.

Later they offered advice.

In the Register of Wills' office, the Registrar expressed his sympathy to the author in four words: "It's hard, isn't it?"

If you are aware of someone who is grieving, how can you let them know you care?

COPING

How does one cope with decisions that have to be made—tasks that have to be taken care of—when you feel you have reached rock bottom and there's no joy left in life? That was the way it was. Each day was a struggle—a struggle to get through the day, and then the long, lonely night. Everyday situations and occurrences that normally would not have been a problem were mountains I did not want to climb. Everything was different now. It seemed there were only bleak, gray days ahead, and I had to face them alone.

I was thankful for the list of "things to do" the funeral director had given me, and during that first week after the funeral I continued to work on those. After registering the will in the Registrar's office, I made an appointment with Lori at the bank to finish making the necessary changes. In addition I called our attorney's office, the office of pensions, and the Social Security office. As I look back, I now see that list of things was a good thing. Although it seemed overwhelming at the time, it gave me a sense of direction, a purpose, a reason for living.

Nevertheless, taking care of a list of "things to do" had its drawbacks. Most of those items on my list had to be taken care of during the day, during normal working hours, generally nine to five. This left all the additional hours of the day open for thinking about Ty, feeling his absence—and thus opening the door for grief to settle heavily upon me. And it did. For me, those first few weeks and months after Ty's death held a pain like no other.

Grief throws that hardest of all hardballs at you, and hits you in your most vulnerable spot . . . and you writhe in pain.

All you want is to have that loved one back again, but you know that is not going to happen. The knowledge that death is final left me with only one hope: the hope that someday I would be able to see Ty again, in Heaven.

It was during the second week following Ty's death that an incident occurred.

* * *

I had just gone to bed for the night and dozed off, when all of a sudden I was awake. I turned over—and there was Ty. He was lying on top of the coverlet, on the opposite side of the bed, where he always slept. Fully dressed, he was wearing the outfit he wore on our first date at Berea—gray tweed slacks and a burgundy vee-neck sweater over a white dress shirt. He was lying on his back, with his head on the pillow, and he looked as though he had just lain down to relax for a few minutes. His eyes were closed, and he did not speak, but he had the most beautiful smile on his face.

"Ty," I exclaimed, "you're really here!"

I started to move toward him—and then he was gone.

* * *

Was this a dream? It was so real, so vivid. Or was Ty really there? Did the Lord, in His goodness, allow Ty to slip through that veil that divides His heavenly world and our earthly one for just a moment or two . . . to comfort me? To let me know that Ty was happy, free of all the indignity and pain he had suffered? I like to think it was the latter. But even if I'm wrong, even if it was only a dream—then the dream came from the Lord. It comforted me and strengthened my hope—hope that is grounded in my faith in the Lord and the promise of eternal life through His death on the cross.

It was to the Lord that I turned during those difficult days. It was the Lord on whom I leaned. And it was from the Lord that I received the greatest comfort. He walked with me through all the pain, all the difficult days and nights. And He walks with me still.

MY GOD IS REAL

It seems the Lord has always been a part of my life. I have memories of my mother kneeling with me beside my bed, even before I started school, teaching me to pray that old familiar children's prayer:

Now I lay me down to sleep; I pray the Lord my soul to keep.
If I should die before I wake, I pray the Lord my soul to take.

During my preschool years a neighbor invited our family to her church, and I had my first visit to Sunday School. I must have been about five at the time, but I remember getting a glimpse of Jesus that day in the preschool class I attended. The teacher held up a picture of Jesus holding a little lamb in His arms. The picture, and the teacher's remarks, all told me that Jesus had to be the most loving, most kind person in the entire world. That impression of the Lord, as viewed in the mind of a little child that Sunday morning, was part of the process of my coming to know God. And my presence in that Sunday School room that morning was part of His plan for me. That image of the Lord is just as bright in my mind today as it was then. I am grateful for that early exposure to the Bible and to the Lord, grateful that I learned at an early age the importance of knowing Him. Even though in the beginning that exposure was through the efforts of others, as I grew, in my heart I felt drawn to the Bible, church, and knowing the Lord. His Word tells us that God has placed in our hearts a desire—a yearning, a need perhaps—and that strong desire, that need, hidden in the deep recesses of our hearts, draws us to Him. In Ecclesiastes 3:11 (NIV) we read:

He has also set eternity in the hearts of men; yet they cannot fathom what God has done from beginning to end.

That yearning was a very real thing for me.

My parents did not attend church, but my mother saw to it that my brother, sister, and I were in church on Sunday mornings—through the kindness of a neighbor. Mrs. Goodnight, a pretty, soft-spoken lady with the sweetest of smiles, lived two houses over with her husband and daughter Barbara Jean. Barbara Jean was a couple of years younger than my little sister Phyllis. Mrs. Goodnight would stop by on Sunday mornings and load the three of us (my brother L.A., Phyllis, and I) into her car and take us to church with her. At first we only attended Sunday church school and worship services. Gradually, as we became older, we became more deeply involved. When I was thirteen I made a commitment to a belief in Christ and expressed a desire to follow His teachings.

The church we attended was Southern Baptist. During those years in which I grew up, Southern Baptist congregations held evangelistic revivals. That usually meant a week of evening services with a visiting evangelist preaching from the pulpit. Each evening, at the end of his message, the evangelist would invite those who did not know the Lord as their Savior to come forward, express repentance for anything they had done that was displeasing to God, and make a commitment to walk in God's way as followers of Jesus.

One evening I watched my brother walk down that aisle.

"Do you want to go to Heaven when your life on earth is ended?" the minister repeated. "Then come to the altar."

"Well, I *definitely* want to go to Heaven when I die," I said to myself. So, as the pianist softly played the plaintive notes of "Amazing Grace," I slipped out of my seat and followed my brother down the aisle.

A few weeks later, one Saturday morning in June, my brother, sister, and I, and several others, were baptized in the St. Jones River, several miles from my home. With baptism I became a full-fledged member of Pleasant View Baptist Church. More important, I had the promise of Heaven and eternal life. The church, which was about a mile from my home, became the center of my social life. There were worship services on Sunday mornings, Baptist Youth Training Union sessions on

Sunday evenings, followed by the minister's second sermon for the day; and, on Wednesday evenings, we had Bible Study and choir practice. I loved it. I loved the feelings, the emotions that were evoked within me when I sat in the sanctuary and listened to words about the Lord. I loved sitting with the choir and singing the old sacred hymns. I loved the church school classes, being taught the Scriptures, and learning about Jesus. I was immersed in the church and quite serious about discipleship and following the Lord.

When I was in high school there was a popular religious song that I loved and would sing over and over. I don't remember the song title, but I remember the words:

My God is real, for I can feel Him in my soul.

That song spoke to me. I loved the melody, I loved the words. The words would run through my mind over and over, and I would find myself singing the song again and again. God was definitely real to me—and that "realness" has remained to this day.

Paradoxically, one of the constants in life is change. Life is continually shifting, and things changed for me when I went away from home and entered Berea College as a student. I allowed other things to slip between God and myself. I began college life at Berea filled with all of those proverbial "good intentions." There was chapel on Sunday evenings with required attendance, and it meant a trip to the Dean's office if we were absent. On Sunday mornings we had the option of attending church services either in the nondenominational Union Church located on campus or in one of the several churches situated in the small town of Berea. I was pleased to find one of the largest churches in town was a Southern Baptist congregation, and I began attending there; after several weeks I joined the church. It wasn't long, however, before the luxury of sleeping late on Sunday mornings, and the demands of homework and study, became excuses for not attending. The church became less and less a part of my life.

But the Lord continued to work in my life to draw me back to the church. And to Himself.

Reflection

Would you say your faith is strong? Why or why not?

If someone asked you how Jesus fits into your life, what would you tell them?

Do you feel church attendance is important? Explain your feelings on this topic.

JOHN GLENN, SPACESHIPS, AND ETERNITY

As I've grown physically and spiritually, I've realized that God uses different means to get our attention and draw us to Himself. For me, it was several different things, but the clincher was . . . a spaceship.

* * *

It was February 1962. The sun was shining, the sky a pastel blue with not a cloud in sight. Excited, I stood in my kitchen and, through the window, searched the heavens. I knew I would not be able to see the spaceship when it launched that morning, but I could imagine . . .

Behind me, in his high chair, eighteen-month-old Darian played with his juice cup and nibbled his graham crackers. *A beautiful day for the launch,* I thought to myself as I glanced over at the clock on the wall. *And it's just about time.*

These were exciting times. America was making her first flights into space.

The names of the first astronauts—Alan Shepard, Gus Grissom, and John Glenn—were becoming household words, heard often over the radio, seen on the front pages of the local newspapers, and tossed around at dinner tables. The first American launched into space, in May 1961, was Shepard. The second, Grissom, flew later that same year.

Those first two flights were of the suborbital variety. Now, on this beautiful February morning in 1962, Astronaut John Glenn was preparing to make the third launch into space. Glenn was destined to become the first American to fully orbit the earth.

I did not want to miss anything, so the radio on the kitchen counter was tuned to NASA, where the launch was broadcast. At the moment a reporter was interviewing Glenn, and one of his questions immediately grabbed my attention. These space flights were pioneer territory, new for the United States, and even though NASA sought to cover all angles, it was reported there was still a possibility that something could go seriously wrong.

"Aren't you afraid," the reporter asked Glenn, "knowing that something unforeseen could happen—and you might not come back alive?"

It was Glenn's answer that gripped me—and wouldn't let go. "No," he answered. "I'm not afraid. I've made my peace with God."

In that instant I realized that . . . if I were in Glenn's situation, I would have been terribly afraid . . . for I did not have that peace in my heart. The peace that comes from knowing that everything is right between you and the Lord. I did not have that assurance, that certainty, that peace of mind about death, and life after death.

* * *

It's history now—the space flight that February morning was successful. John Glenn *did* come back alive. He went on to become a United States Senator. But for me, Glenn's words that morning were a wake-up call. I had gotten completely away from the church. In college at Berea, and then after Ty and I were married, though we both were Christians, neither of us made a place in our lives for the Lord. And I had been feeling guilty—each time we drove by a church, and especially on Sunday mornings when the church bells rang—for I knew I should be there. A few weeks later, after Glenn's flight into space, I began attending First Baptist Church of Harrisonburg, Virginia, where we lived; the door was opened to allow the Lord back into my life. God used that space flight, and Glenn's words that February morning, to draw me back into the church and to Himself.

* * *

So it was only natural that, at this time in my life, after the death of my husband, I would turn to the Lord. Each evening I sat at the kitchen table, my Bible open before me, and made an attempt to keep up with my daily Bible reading. My method for reading the Scriptures has always been to read straight through the Bible, a number of chapters each day. However, during all the months of Ty's illness, my Bible reading had been neglected. And now it was difficult. I could not concentrate. I could not seem to move beyond the present and the pain I was experiencing. My thoughts always turned to Ty and how much I missed him, and the tears would start. Yet, I knew that, in the Lord's omniscience, I could pour out all my pain and sorrow, my loneliness, my feelings of desperation, and it would be okay—for He already knew. He knew how I was feeling and what I would say. We are told in the Scriptures that He knows every thought—and every word—even before we speak:

> *O Lord, you have searched me and you know me.*
> *You know when I sit and when I rise; you perceive my*
> *thoughts from afar . . . Before a word is on my tongue, you*
> *know it completely, O Lord (Psalm 139:1, 2, 4, NIV).*

This Scripture was comforting. It was comforting to know that the Lord knew my thoughts, that He knew how I was feeling. The Scripture told me that I did not need to put my feelings into Words, for He knew, He understood. And at times it was enough just to sit silently in His presence. Even though my situation did not change, even though the pain and heartache did not go away, I felt comforted in my pain.

It was during the second week after the funeral, as I struggled to cope with everything, that I remembered Pastor Roland Coon's words to me as he was leaving the funeral service. "We have a grief support group in Calvary Church, and they are just beginning a new thirteen-week session. You may want to give the group a try."

A grief support group . . . surely I wouldn't need that . . . I thought. And so I thanked him, yet tucked his words away in my heart. But now I was miserable. I was lonely. And things were not getting any better. I decided to give the grief support group a visit.

Reflection

On the night Jesus was born, shepherds in the field, keeping watch over their sheep, were the first to hear of His birth.

Do you remember when you first heard about Jesus? How old were you? Where were you?

How did the news make you feel?

FINDING SUPPORT

Group therapy. I had read about support groups and seen them portrayed on television (mostly Alcoholics Anonymous groups), but I knew little about them. Nevertheless, with the nudging in my heart to at least check this group out, I visited the grief support group at the church the following Tuesday.

There was snow on the ground and the temperature was hovering around freezing, but inside the church I found warmth and comfort. The room we were meeting in was small and usually used as a place for prayer. Comfortable chairs and a love seat lined the wall for the nine individuals who were there that evening. I had not notified anyone that I would be there, so the participants, all of whom were strangers to me, were surprised to see me.

This group was an arm of the worldwide GriefShare Program and Ministry, a network of grief recovery and support groups for those mourning the death of a loved one. The thirteen-week program is biblically based, and this group met once each week for about two hours.

During those two hours a video was shown, one relating to the particular theme for the evening, followed by discussion of the video and any other needs the group might wish to discuss. There was also a workbook with meaningful Scriptures and questions to ponder for each of the thirteen sessions, plus meditations or readings for the participants to use each evening at home. The group met on Tuesdays from 6:30 to 8:30 PM.

The number in attendance varied each week, as some could not attend, or chose not to attend, each session. Three of the other ladies in the group had recently lost their husbands. There was Peggy, an older lady whose husband had passed away a week or so before, Tracey, and Sue. Tracey's husband had passed away about three years earlier, and Sue was a young mother who was there with her eight-year-old daughter. Sue's husband had recently died from cancer. In addition, there was a couple mourning the death of their adult son, and a woman who had lost her mother. And then there was Ella.

A stranger, Ella sat beside me at the meeting that cold, wintry January evening. It was two weeks following my husband's funeral. We were asked to introduce ourselves and explain why we were there. Ella was there, she said, because she had lost her son. My wound was too fresh, too raw . . . I could not speak about my loss; I could only weep. After the session ended, Ella came over to me, wrapped her arms around me, pulled me close, and we wept, sharing our suffering. I will never forget Ella: her warm, caring hug melted a little of the ice that had formed around my heart and truly comforted me.

I continued to meet with the group, and I continued to be bolstered and encouraged each week. It helped just to be there, just to see that I was not alone in my grief. It helped to be among others who understood exactly how I was feeling and how deeply I was hurting, for they were hurting too. In that little prayer room we could cry, we could let our feelings hang out. We were something like icicles on the branch of a tree in a freezing rain. And like icicles that melt in warmth, and as they melt they blend together, we shared our suffering in our grief and we bonded, helping each other heal. Frederick Buechner, noted author, minister, educator, and philosopher, in his book *Now and Then* writes:

> *To suffer in love for another's suffering is to live life not only at its fullest but at its holiest.*[2]

I dare say his words perfectly describe our grief support group as we shared our suffering each week.

As we met together each week, we learned a great deal about grief and the grieving process. And one of the first requirements for healing from grief, we learned, is that those of us who are grieving must accept the fact that our loved one is gone from our lives, that he or she is never going to return. We must accept the fact that our life is never going to be as it was before. And this isn't easy to do. We may know that the one we love is no longer here, but we don't want this to be true. And some may temporarily block that hard-to-accept truth out of their consciousness. (Our minds use various means of protecting us.) But eventually we must face the truth—we must face reality.

There is a plaque on the wall above my husband's desk which bears these words from St. Francis of Assisi:

> *God grant me the serenity*
> *to accept the things*

I cannot change,
courage to change the things
I can, and the wisdom
to know the difference.

St. Francis's words about acceptance form a beautiful and appropriate prayer for those of us who grieve.

The support group helped immensely. Each time we shared about ourselves and our loss, each time I talked about losing Ty, the cold, hard truth would sink in a little deeper. That helped me accept the reality. For me, however, and for some of the others, sharing was difficult. It wasn't until the fourth or fifth week that I was able to talk about losing Ty. Nevertheless, everyone seemed to understand, and there was never any criticism. Everyone was supportive.

That's the beauty of the GriefShare program: no one is pushed to talk about their loss, or to speak at all, until they are ready. Nevertheless, most of those who are quiet in the beginning eventually want to talk about their loved one and their loss, and then they are ready to share.

MISSING YOU

You have gone
and left me here alone

to face the lonely days
of pain and heartache.

I never knew
how empty life could be

without you here with me.
I miss you so.

My tears I can't contain
at the whisper of your name;

my heart is pained
and memories flood my soul,

of yesterday and you
and things we used to do.

I miss you so.

The sun will rise each morn,
and evening shadows come and go;

but life will never be
as it was for you and me;

for my life, you know, was you.

I miss you so.

GRIEF'S EMOTIONAL ROLLER COASTER

Support groups may not be for everyone, but I highly recommend to all who are grieving the loss of a loved one that they consider joining a grief support group. GriefShare provides great support, and there are other grief support groups as well. Hospice, for instance, provides end of life care as well as grief support, and often churches and local hospitals offer grief support as part of their health care program. GriefShare carried me through those first few painful weeks and months after Ty's death, and after my healing I remained with the group and served as a counselor/facilitator. I was fortunate that my church had the program. Without that support, I believe my healing would have taken much longer.

GriefShare was valuable for me in many ways. Topping the list would be that I gained a better understanding of grief—what it involves and how it affects us. It seems grief is a subject most of us do not think about, at all, until it hits home personally. Until we lose someone we love. But isn't that logical? Why think about something so depressing and unpopular as grief unless we have to? Nevertheless, when someone we love dies, *suddenly we are there . . . struggling, lost . . . walking the long, lonely road of grief.* We walk blindly on that road of grief, struggling with shock and the pain of our loss, not knowing what to expect, rejecting reality—we don't want the death to be real. And then, barraged with a flood of emotions that have to be dealt with, we find ourselves on grief's emotional roller coaster. As a child growing up in a rural area of a small town in the North Carolina mountains, I always looked forward to the time when the carnival would come to town with its assortment of rides—the gentle merry-go-round; the quiet, dependable Ferris wheel; the speedy, exciting roller coaster; and various other rides.

"C'mon, let's go ride the roller coaster!" eventually someone would cry. "Not me!" *would be my response. "Not that one, with its high speed, its super height, those ups and downs . . . It's too scary for me!"*

But now I had been forced to ride grief's emotional roller coaster.

In grief we have our ups and downs, our good days and bad days, our sudden stops and starts. We have those times when we feel okay; we are rolling along at a nice, comfortable speed when suddenly we find ourselves hurtling downhill, and soon we're at the bottom again. The grief ride is an uncomfortable ride, one no one wants to take . . . but with grief we don't get to say no.

In grief, some try to avoid dealing with their emotions. Some withdraw and try to isolate themselves, not going out, not answering the phone. Attempting, perhaps, not to have to deal with the situation, or perhaps to keep from feeling the pain. But emotions need to be dealt with. Research has shown that if we bury feelings and suppress them, they remain buried inside us and can resurface at a later time, possibly causing problems.

In the grief support group we were encouraged to envelop our feelings and not suppress them. We were encouraged . . . to remember, to *feel* (cry if we felt like crying, talk about him or her if we felt like talking about him or her), and to give expression to what we were feeling, possibly in these ways:

- by keeping a journal

- writing a letter to the one who is no longer here

- writing out our prayers, or a letter to the Lord

- or through expressing how we are feeling in a poem.

I did all of the above, with one exception: I did not write a letter to Ty. I journaled; I wrote out my prayers, telling the Lord exactly how I was feeling. I talked about Ty and our life together with others, more often with family. I looked at photo albums when I longed to see him, and I expressed how I felt in poems. In doing these things my feelings of pain and loneliness were released instead of being suppressed, and this was good. It's important that those who are grieving realize the emotions they're feeling are normal and need to be dealt with. They don't just go away, and burying them might only lead to problems later on.

Research has shown that what affects one the most may not affect others in the same way. In the grief support group I found the emotions that tended to be the most difficult were loneliness, anger, guilt, and depression. And topping the list was . . . loneliness. This was especially true for those who had lost their spouse, as I had. *"I feel that part of me has been ripped away.*" This was the cry I heard over and over from individuals who had lost their spouse. These words speak to the close relationship between husbands and wives and help explain the depth of the pain.

The vows we take at our wedding tend to meld two people into one entity, and we think of those two in that way—as one. And then, when one is taken away, half of the entity is gone.

Henceforth the cry, "I feel like half of me has been ripped away."

In February, about a month after Ty's funeral, I changed doctors. In filling out the forms that are necessary for first-time patients, I was shocked when I read the question related to marital status and saw only two options: married or single. It was upsetting, first of all because there were only the two options, and I did not feel I fit into either one! Second, it once again forced me to face my new reality. Even though I was now single (so to speak), it was a different kind of "single" than someone who has never married or, perhaps, is divorced. I wrestled with my thoughts.

What do I say? I'm not really married now—I don't have a husband any longer, and I don't feel single. What do I do?

This simple question jolted me into the realization that my status in life had truly changed. Finally, I drew a line through the word *married* and wrote above it *widow*, and then I added: *as of December 29, 2009.*

A second jolt came a little later when the doctor asked if I was depressed. I reacted with a firm "No," for I had not thought of myself as depressed. But in that moment, I realized the word *depressed* described my situation perfectly, that how

I was feeling fit directly into the definition of the word: *low in spirits, dejected, sad.* So I added, "Well, I suppose that I am." This experience helped me see that as a rule others expect those who are grieving the loss of a loved one to be depressed. The problem is, in our pain and sadness, the pain is so intense we cannot analyze our condition, we can only feel.

My life at this point was just one big, gray, gloomy painful area. And into that area, along with the pain and suffering, the loneliness and depression, tagging along were guilt and confusion.

CONFUSION

It was almost 11 o'clock, the time for my appointment. I pushed open the door and entered the dentist's waiting room. The receptionist opened the glass window above her desk, smiled, and said, "May I help you?"

"Yes, I'm here for my appointment," I replied, and stated my name.

The receptionist looked down at her desk for a brief moment, then, smiling broadly, she said, "Your appointment isn't until tomorrow."

This took place in February, just more than a month after Ty's death. There was a similar incident a week or so before this when the daughter of a friend of mine passed away. That Saturday afternoon when I arrived for the memorial service, I was surprised to find the parking lot empty and the building locked. When I returned home and checked the obituary notice, I saw that I was a week early; the service was scheduled for the following Saturday! These personal faux pas were embarrassing, and under other circumstances I might have smiled about them, because memorial services and sitting in the dentist's chair are two of my least favorite things.

There were also occasions when I would be driving down a street, my mind on Ty and not on my driving, when suddenly I would be jolted into the present by this thought: *My goodness, where am I?*

It was surprising—yet also a relief—to learn that confusion can be a part of the grieving process. My confusion was related to time. My days seemed to meld into each other, and it was difficult to keep track of which day of the week it was, which month we were in, or my appointments with the doctor, dentist, and others. Chris Ann Waters captures the essence of time, for those who grieve, in her book *Seasons of Goodbye*. She writes, "Suns and moons spill over each other and time takes on a strange new meaning. Time is not."[3] Basically, for me, as far as time was concerned, as to what time it was, what day it was—it just did not matter. Even so, it was a great relief to learn that such things as I was experiencing were considered normal for those walking the road of grief.

ANGER AND GUILT

"I was angry!" he said. "I left the hospital that evening under the impression that everything was going to be all right, that my wife was going to be all right. Then, when I came in the next day . . .

"'We're sorry, but your wife passed away,' they said.

"Believe me, I was angry! They said she would be okay—or I would have been there . . ."

Anger and guilt. These were two other emotions often evident among those in the grief support group. There were some who were angry at the doctor or others in the hospital for allowing their loved one to die. This man's account is a good example. Some were angry at family members for various reasons. Some were angry at themselves. Some were angry at God. And some, it seemed, were just angry. This too is considered normal among those who are grieving. And it was always rewarding to see that anger dissipate as time moved on, to see those angry ones discover the reason for their anger, begin to deal with it, and let it go.

Accompanying anger is guilt. Often anger and guilt blend together, as in those times when someone becomes angry at himself or herself for something they felt they should have done, but didn't do . . . as was true for me. It was not anger I felt, but guilt. Guilt for not being with my husband when he passed away. Perhaps my lack of anger was due to the fact that Ty was sick for such a long time before his death. We knew what was coming, and that gave us time to prepare for it emotionally and physically. Guilt, however, was a different matter altogether.

Oh, God, please let me be with Ty when you call him home.

This short prayer was one I prayed over and over. I wanted so much to be with Ty when he drew his last breath. I did not want him to be alone. And so I prayed, and I prayed . . . but . . . my prayer was not answered the way I hoped it would be.

As the summer of 2009 slipped into fall and then winter, it became more and more obvious that Ty was not going to recover from his health issues. I did not want this to be true.

I pushed all of those little nagging thoughts deep into my subconscious mind and avoided the truth. Eventually, however, my self-subterfuge failed, and I had to face the fact that I was losing him. And then I began to pray:

Lord, please let me be with him when the time comes, when you call him home.

I wanted so much that he not be alone at that time, and even more, I wanted to be there by his side, holding his hand. But that did not happen.

On that last day, when I learned that Ty's death would be soon, I called the family to let them know. The hospital wanted to move him to a different room. Perhaps to a larger room, one more suitable for family members to gather. But apparently there was nowhere to go; all their beds were full and there were no rooms available. Later that morning a representative from Hospice came in and suggested moving him to Hospice Care. I finally, reluctantly agreed to do that, and preparations for the move began. But then I had to leave. Our daughter Tara was on her way down from Wilmington, and I needed be at home when she arrived. She did not have a key to the house and I had no way to contact her. Moreover, December 29 was one of those exceptionally cold days; the temperature was below freezing. This meant leaving Ty. I struggled. I did not want to leave Ty—and I am sure I was not thinking clearly—but I could not think of any other solution except to go home and be there when Tara arrived.

Ty was heavily sedated, of course, so I whispered in his ear.

"Ty, I have to leave. Tara is coming down and I have to go
home for a few minutes. But I will be back.
I will see you in a little while."

Those were my last words to my husband.

It was only a short time later, while I was home, that the phone call came.

* * *

"Hello."

"Mrs. Tisinger. I'm the nurse here with your husband, and he is only seconds from passing . . . We need your permission to remove the breathing tube."

"Oh, no!" I literally screamed this into the phone. My thoughts were in a tangle. "I wanted to be with him . . . "

"The chaplain is here with him now, and we need your permission to remove the breathing tube."

"I'm coming down," I yelled into the phone, slamming the receiver.

* * *

By the time I arrived, Ty was gone.

Why? Why, Lord? Why could I not have been with him? I kept asking these questions. *Why? Why could he not have lived just a little while longer until I could be with him?* I was not angry with God. I was disappointed and angry with myself—that I was not with Ty.

These questions tormented me during the days and weeks after the funeral. Finally, one morning I picked up the phone, called the Hospice Center, and asked to speak with the nurse who was with Ty when he died. I needed to know about his last moments. I explained how I had wanted to be with him, but couldn't, and how I had prayed over and over that the Lord would allow me to be with him when the time came. Her answer surprised me.

"Did you ever stop to think that was not what the Lord had in mind?" she asked. "No," was my soft, one-word answer. My only thought had been of myself, what *I* wanted to happen.

The counselor's words that day gave me a peace in my heart that had long been absent.

Her words helped me be able to accept not being with Ty during the last moments of his life. Her words helped me see that the way things happened was not entirely up to me, that our loving God was in charge. God was in control, and perhaps there was a reason for my not being there. Later I came to realize that our loving God, in his infinite grace and mercy, *had* (in a way) allowed me to be with Ty. He arranged that phone call from the nurse *only seconds from Ty's passing.*

On my path along this road of grief, I have found there are others who, for one reason or another, are not able to be with their loved one at the moment of their passing. And most always, others who are left behind, as I was, are left with a deep sadness and either anger or remorse. That day in early March, as I spoke to the nurse at Hospice, she also said that she and others who work with those who are dying have learned that often the person who is dying will wait until the wife or husband, friend or other family member, leaves their side for a few minutes (perhaps for a bathroom break); that is when they slip away. Those words also helped relieve the guilt I was feeling and added peace to my heart.

Reflection

Is there a "Why?" that has been troubling you?

Is there someone (a doctor, a nurse, your pastor) you could turn to for help?

But always—and foremost—pray.

PART VII

BEGINNING ANEW

*It is of the Lord's mercies
that we are not consumed,
because his compassions fail not.
They are new every morning:
great is thy faithfulness.*

LAMENTATIONS 3:22, 23 (KJV)

PICKING UP THE PIECES

The death of a loved one is a life-shattering event for those whose lives are touched by it. Losing someone we love leaves a big hole, a huge empty space in our lives, and any feeling of peace and contentment, even our sense of security, can be thrown into disarray. That's the situation in which most of us who grieve the death of a loved one eventually find ourselves. But we cannot let it stay that way. Life continues, and we must move with it or risk sinking further into grief's grasp or becoming stuck in our grief. Eventually we have to pick up the pieces of our broken lives and try to fit everything together again.

In my grief support group, the program we used (as I wrote, called GriefShare) was biblically based, and Scripture constituted a major portion of our study as we progressed in our journey toward healing. Appropriate Scriptures were used weekly to encourage, enlighten, support, and help us heal. One of the Scriptures referenced was the story of two sisters, Mary and Martha, and the death of their brother Lazarus. I had read this story many times over the years, but when I saw it through the eyes of grief, the story took on new significance. I have learned that as we read and study the Bible, the Lord gives us insight and understanding of His truths (as we need them and are ready to receive them). I found the biblical account of Mary and Martha and the death of their brother Lazarus, at this time in my life, faith-strengthening. In it the Lord shows His loving care for those who grieve.

Reflection

AT HOME IN BETHANY
(A Scene, Imagined)

"How is he this morning, Martha? Has he shown any improvement?" Mary wanted so much to hear good news—news that their brother Lazarus was feeling better.

Martha's look of helplessness and worry spoke volumes to her sister. "No, Mary. I see none. In fact, he seems a little worse."

Mary moved to stand beside the pallet on which her brother lay; she placed her hand gently on his forehead. "Ummm . . . he's still very warm . . . but I don't know what more we can do. We're giving him all the herbs and medicine we were told to give him. Maybe we should send word to Rabbi."

Martha turned to face her sister. "I worry greatly, Mary. Our brother has been sick for so long now—and still there's no sign that he's getting better."

A faint moan came from the man lying on the pallet. He moved his head feverishly from side to side, but his eyes remained closed. Martha picked up a small linen cloth from the table next to the pallet, dipped it in the water in the earthen bowl on the table, and gently sponged her brother's forehead. "Do you not see, Mary? He's been this way most of the night."

Mary placed her hand on Martha's arm. "Yes," she said. "We must let Rabbi know that the one He loves is sick. We must send word to Rabbi, to Jesus."

MARY, MARTHA, AND ME

In the New Testament, in the Gospel of John, we learn that Mary, Martha, and Lazarus were friends of Jesus. The Scriptures tell us that at one point Lazarus became very ill, and Mary and Martha sent word to Jesus,

"Lord, the one you love is sick" (John 11:3, NIV).

Apparently Mary and Martha believed that Jesus would come directly to their home when He received their message that Lazarus was ill. But when Jesus received the news, He intentionally delayed going to Bethany. As recorded in John, He said to His disciples:

"This sickness will not end in death. No, it is for God's glory so that God's Son may be glorified through it"(John 11:4, NIV).

Jesus knew what was ahead—that Lazarus *would* die. But He also knew that Lazarus would be restored to life, and in his restoration God would be glorified. And so Jesus, who was a day's travel away, delayed going to Mary and Martha's home for two days. When He did arrive, Lazarus had been dead for four days. According to the Scriptures, when Jesus arrived and saw how Mary and Martha and the others were weeping and mourning Lazarus's death, He was deeply troubled. And He wept (John 11:35).

Jesus wept. Jesus—the Son of God—wept. He was the Christ, the Messiah. He was Emanuel, God with us. And He knew what would be happening. He *knew* that Lazarus was going to walk out of that tomb shortly and be alive again. He *knew* He was going to call Lazarus's name and Lazarus would come forth out of that tomb. But still, He wept. Why? Because He cared. Because He saw how Mary and Martha and the others were hurting, and He felt *their* pain. This Scripture tells us that our heavenly Father cares when we grieve, that He cares deeply, that He feels our pain. And just as Jesus was there with Mary and Martha and their friends when Lazarus died, He is near to those of us who mourn and seek His presence today.

Jesus revealed important truths that day in Bethany, truths about God and His marvelous love. Truths that were meant not only for Mary and Martha and their friends, but for all who have lost someone they love. Truths that are significant to those of us who grieve today.

First, we can be sure the Lord is aware of our situation—and our grief. When Jesus received the news from Mary and Martha that Lazarus was ill, He intentionally delayed going to the home of His friends to minister to Lazarus and make him well. Of course, He could have healed Lazarus without going to their home; Jesus did not need to be physically present to heal him. But He did not do so. And then Lazarus died. Jesus knew that Lazarus had died, but He also knew the bigger picture; he knew God's larger plan. He said to His disciples:

*"Lazarus is dead, and for your sake I am glad that
I was not there, so that you may believe. But let
us go to him" (John 11:14, 15, NIV).*

Jesus' words—*"I am glad for your sake that I was not
there"*—are important. Jesus knew that Mary and Martha
hoped that He would come and heal their brother. But He
also knew the end result: Lazarus would die, but he would
live again. And through his resurrection, God the Father and
God the Son would be glorified. So the delay was necessary.
However, Jesus was aware that Mary and Martha were hurting; He was aware of their grief and their need. When the
time was right, He went to their home. Likewise, when we
are grieving we can be sure the Lord is aware of our situation,
that He knows our pain. We can be sure He knows the extent
of our grief, and that He waits close by, ready to comfort and
sustain us.

Second, Jesus ministered to Mary and Martha personally
and individually. When Martha heard that Jesus was coming, she went out to meet Him, and He talked with her and
comforted her. Mary stayed at the house. However, after Jesus
spoke with Martha, He sent for Mary. This reveals an important point. The Lord was present; He was near, and He wanted
to comfort Mary. Why, then, did He not go to the house to
find Mary and comfort her there? Instead, He asked that she
come to Him. (According to the Scriptures, Jesus was just
outside the village, in the place where Martha had met Him.)
The Bible doesn't give us a specific answer to this question.
Perhaps it was simply that it was important that Mary leave
other distractions behind. Perhaps it was because it is the
Lord's desire that we seek Him—that we come to Him in our

distress as Martha had done. Nevertheless, He longs to comfort us; He reaches out to us. When our hearts are broken and we mourn, the Lord is near, patiently waiting for us to seek Him. He comforted both Mary and Martha individually and personally. *Will He not do the same for you and me?*

Third, He bears our pain. Jesus showed the caring heart of God that day in Bethany. He not only ministered to both Mary and Martha—He answered their questions and offered comfort—also, out of His compassion, He grieved with them. He *wept* with them. What greater example could we have that God feels our pain and cares?

Fourth, He turned their mourning into joy when He called, "Lazarus, come out!" Lazarus walked out of that tomb restored to life. This is, to all of us who believe in the Lord, a *promise illustrated*—a promise of life after death, of the truth locked in the promise that our loved ones also will emerge from death's tomb and live again.

* * *

There are other examples in the Bible in which Jesus brings the dead back to life, including the twelve-year-old daughter of Jairus, a leader in the synagogue (Luke, chapter 8) and the son of the widow of Nain (Luke, chapter 7). In both instances we see the Lord's compassion and love.

Jairus

Jairus was a synagogue ruler. He came to Jesus and asked that He go to his home and heal his daughter, who was dying. While Jesus was on the way to Jairus's home, Jairus's servants came out to meet him to tell him that his daughter had died.

When Jesus heard this, he said, "Don't be afraid; just believe, and she will be healed." Then, when he arrived at Jairus's house, Jesus took the child by the hand and said, "My child, get up!" At once, she stood up.

The Widow of Nain

In the second instance, Jesus happened upon a funeral procession.

It was for the only son of a widow who lived in the town of Nain. We see Jesus' compassion in these words.

When the Lord saw her, his heart went out to her and he said, "Don't cry" (Luke 7:13, NIV).

Then Jesus touched the coffin and commanded the young man to get up, and the widow's son was restored to life.

* * *

Jesus' ministry that day in Bethany was for Mary, Martha . . . and me. And for all who grieve. From this example we can know that *God is aware of our grief, that He is near, that He cares, and that He shares our grief, He weeps with us.* But, most important, we can know that death is not the end, that there is life after death, that we will again see our loved ones who believe in the Lord.

Reflection

THE TOMB AT BETHANY
(A Scene, Imagined; John 11:19-36 [NIV, paraphrased])

Many Jews had come to Martha and Mary to comfort them in the loss of their brother.

Jesus and his disciples had just arrived. They were just outside the village. "Look!" one of the mourners yelled. "It's the Nazarene! It's Rabbi! We must let Mary and Martha know." Immediately, this friend ran to tell them.

When Martha heard that Jesus was coming, she hurried out to meet him. "Lord," she said. "If you had been here, my brother would not have died." Her eyes filled with tears. "But I know that even now God will give you whatever you ask."

Jesus placed his hand upon her shoulder. "Martha, Martha," he said. "Your brother will rise again."

"Yes, I know he will rise again in the resurrection at the last day . . . " Martha wiped her eyes on the sleeve of her garment.

"I am the resurrection and the life," Jesus continued. "He who believes in me will live, even though he dies; and whoever lives and believes in me will never die. Do you believe this?"

"Yes, Lord," Martha told him. "I believe that you are the Christ, the Son of God who was to come into the world."

When Jesus asked about Mary, who had stayed at home, Martha hurried to get her.

"The Teacher is here," Martha said to Mary, "and is asking for you." Mary got up quickly and went out to go to him. When the Jews who had been with Mary in the house noticed how

quickly she got up and went out, they followed, supposing she was going to the tomb to mourn there.

When Mary reached Jesus, she fell at his feet. Weeping, she said, "Lord, if you had been here, my brother would not have died."

When Jesus saw her weeping, and the Jews who had come along with her also weeping, he was deeply moved in spirit and troubled. "Where have you laid him?" he asked.

"Come and see, Lord," they replied. Jesus wept. Then the Jews said, "See how he loved him!"

I'M LEARNING
TO LIVE WITH . . .

THE LONELINESS

Lottie was a spiritual mentor for me and one of my closest friends. Lottie and Harold had been married for more than half a century when Harold passed away. "I'm so lonely," Lottie said often, to me and others. She was always so glad to have me stop by for just a visit, to run an errand for her, or to pick her up for a church service or some other event. She always appreciated my presence, even something as small as a brief phone call.

Now I understand. Now, like Lottie, I too am a widow, and like Lottie, part of me is missing. Before my husband died, I had companionship—now loneliness is my companion. I saw my husband as my best friend, my protector, my confidant, my helper. He was my chauffeur, my accountant, my mechanic, my gardener, my light bulb changer, and on and on. He was the one, other than the Lord, who shared that most secret place in my heart. And now he's gone.

THE EMPTY BED AT NIGHT

Night, for me, was the most difficult time. I can still feel the chill, that icy coldness that enveloped me as I walked into our bedroom the night of Ty's death. The emptiness hit me like a sudden blast of Arctic wind. In remembering, it all comes back . . . that feeling of despair as I turned back the covers on the bed . . . the pain in my heart . . . the tears . . . That was the first night of many.

In addition, I always had a fear of being alone, and now for the first time in my life I was truly alone. That first night, the night of Ty's death, the lights in the house were not turned off. I had to be able to see . . . I could not be alone in the dark. I even stayed up to a later hour so that I would have less time to spend in bed.

And then there was the sleeplessness. There were some nights in which, I am sure, I did not sleep at all. And I have heard from other women who have lost their husbands, and men who have lost their wives, that not being able to sleep is a common problem.

THE EMPTY CHAIR ACROSS THE TABLE

Eating was another problem. I really didn't care about meals, about what I ate. I kept to the schedule—breakfast, lunch, and dinner—out of habit, and I ate because I knew it was necessary. Sitting there and staring at that empty chair across the table was painful. It was another reminder that Ty was gone, that things would never be the same. Even though in the last few months of Ty's life that chair had been empty because he was spending most of his day in bed, *he was there.* And now the bedroom was as empty as that chair across the table. There was no one for whom to make that special dish or that special dessert. There was no one to taste the new recipe, smile, and say, "Hey, this is really good!" There was no one to help me prepare for those special occasions, or help me clean up afterward, as Ty usually did.

Shopping for groceries was another area that required adjustment. Ty and I often shopped together as many couples do; now I wandered up and down the aisles alone with my shopping cart. In the store I would catch myself looking on the shelves for his favorite foods, then I would remember and say to myself, "Hey, you don't need that anymore, he's gone."

In those first weeks and months I ate a lot of soup and sandwiches. Often I bought foods and carried them home, with good intentions. But in my distress, more often than not, the foods had to be thrown out because they spoiled in the refrigerator or grew too old to be edible.

THE QUIET SOUND OF NOTHINGNESS

Marge was another good friend who lost her husband. "You know what I do now?" she asked me one day. "I put a disc in the record player and turn the volume up as loud as I can." At the time I wondered about that. *Why would she want to do such a thing?* But, as it was with Lottie, now I understand.

The house is so quiet now. There's no one to make noise but myself. There's no one with whom to talk, to share that funny little anecdote, or to say, "Hey, we have a problem here. What are we going to do about it?" There's no one to talk to about that slow drip in the kitchen faucet or that nagging pain in my shoulder.

Just as Marge did, I made adjustments, I made noise. I would turn on the television and watch the news, or sometimes a movie—if it wasn't a comedy. I didn't feel like laughing. But I could easily get a good cry out of a sad drama or a romance that had gone bad. And at times I would even catch myself commenting to Ty, just as though he were there with me . . .

Ty did not like me to watch him do repair work around the house. One time when he had to change the filter in the kitchen faucet, I watched. He frowned at me because I was watching.

A couple of months after the funeral, the filter in the kitchen faucet needed changing; I was hesitant to do it because I had never changed the filter before.

But I found it was not really difficult. I was successful, and I felt really proud of myself. I turned around, as though Ty were standing there, and said, "See, Ty, if I had not watched you, I would not have known how to do this."

When I was a child, I remember reading, or hearing about, older people who talked to themselves, or to someone who was not there—and I laughed. I thought it was funny. And now I was that person. But I've learned I'm not alone in this respect; I have learned that others who are grieving talk to their missing partner just as I did. And that's okay.

Yes, Lottie, loneliness is difficult to deal with—as are confusion, anger, guilt, and all the many other emotions we face when we lose someone we love. But we have to adjust—we have no choice but to adjust—if we want to be healed.

Reflection

ADJUSTING

I'm learning to live with the loneliness;
the empty bed at night,
the empty chair across the table,
and the quiet sound of nothingness
where once was light and life.

But there are times when the solitary
cuts like a knife,
and I cannot help but unlock the door
of remembering;
knowing full well the pain that will come
in seeing your smile,
and hearing your voice,
and imagining your arms holding me tight,
safe, protected, loved.

If only . . .
If only the moment could last.
But then, you're gone, and
I'm left alone in my room,
full, yet empty.

PART VIII

LIFE GOES ON

Generations come and generations go,
but the earth remains forever.
The sun rises and the sun sets,
and hurries back to where it rises.
The wind blows to the south
and turns to the north;
round and round it goes,
ever returning on its course.

ECCLESIASTES 1:4-6 (NIV)

WHEN?

"You keep saying things will get better—
that the pain will go away. When? . . .
When do we reach that point that our pain goes away?"

When I first joined the grief support group there were mostly women attending; there was only one gentleman, a husband there with his wife. They were mourning the death of their son, who had been in his early twenties and passed away suddenly. Several months later a gentleman joined the group who had recently lost his wife. His tears were copious, and one night, with tears streaming down his face, he asked, "When do we reach that point that our pain goes away?"

We could not answer his question. We had no answer . . . except that healing *will come,* and that healing varies from person to person. This man stayed with the group and continued to participate, and I dare say that healing did come for him—as it did for me. However, he learned, as we all did, that the pain of losing someone you love never goes away. We simply learn to live with it.

* * *

It was a Sunday in December 2010. One year following Ty's death. I was at church that evening for a memorial service. The service was sponsored by the church's GriefShare committee for those who had lost a loved one during the year.

We were invited to bring a larger photograph of our loved one and place it on the stage with other photographs. I was scheduled to do a reading in the program and was seated on the front pew, possibly eight to ten feet from the stage. As I sat there, staring at my husband's photo, the huge, empty space between us, suddenly it hit me.

He's "over there," and I'm "over here."
He's in Heaven, and I'm down here.
There's a great divide between us; we can no longer touch.

It had been a year since my husband's death, but still that realization caused an avalanche of tears. No, the pain never goes away.

* * *

More than ten years have slipped by since that December night at the memorial service described above, and I can still say, "No, the pain never goes away." In March 2009 the popular actor and film star, Liam Neeson, lost his wife, Natalia Richardson. She was fatally injured on a ski slope. In an article in *Parade Magazine*, dated April 24, 2022, thirteen years after his wife's death, Neeson apparently agreed. Talking about his wife's death, he said, "You can put grief away, you can push it to a corner, but it's always there."[1]

That December evening in 2010, one year after Ty's death, comfort came from those around me, and in being reminded of God's promises as we comforted each other in our grief. God, in His infinite love and mercy, offers healing, comfort, and hope. He offers healing from our grief and the promise of eternal life through Jesus' death on the cross for those who trust in Him. This is our comfort and source of hope: one day we will be able to see our loved one again. Along with healing, if we allow Him to do so, the Lord will carry us through the pain, loneliness, and sleepless nights and walk with us each step of the way into the new life (a sort of new normal) death has forced us into. No matter how long it takes.

Reflection

He tends his flock like a shepherd:
He gathers the lambs in his arms
and carries them close to his heart.
Isaiah 40:11 (NIV)

These words of the prophet Isaiah paint a beautiful picture of the Lord holding us, his people, close to his heart and carrying us as a shepherd carries a little lamb.

These words inspire comfort and trust. Think of a time when the Lord carried you. Give Him thanks.

NEVER ONCE DID
I WALK ALONE

Little did I know that Sunday evening in December 2010, as I sat in the church at the memorial service and stared at my husband's photo, what the coming year had in store for me. And little did I know that in the coming year I was to see, even more clearly, the Lord's great care for me.

* * *

"You didn't bring someone with you?" The doctor's gaze met mine.

She's not smiling . . . A red flag shot up. Perched on the edge of the examining table, I pulled my pink exam jacket closer around my bare chest. "I didn't have anyone to bring," I replied.

Turning toward the desk behind her, the doctor stated, "We have your biopsy report. You have cancer."

Stunned, I glanced at the nurse. Her eyes never left my face. The doctor continued, "The biopsy shows that you have stage one ductal carcinoma in the left breast. These are your options . . . "

Cancer! That's not what I'm supposed to hear! Shock held me motionless. I had been telling myself: *It's probably just a cyst. No one in my family has had cancer. I'm sure I will be told everything is fine.* But those were not the words I just heard.

Later, I left the doctor's office still trying to grasp the full extent of what lay ahead: surgery in two weeks to remove the cancer and any affected lymph nodes, then radiation treatment. *And then what? Chemotherapy? A number of my friends had faced this—and some did not survive. Had I just been given a death sentence as well?*

I recalled all the times I walked with my husband through his biopsies, diagnoses, surgeries, and recoveries before his death one year earlier. "All those times I was with him, Lord," I prayed, "and now I have to go through this alone."

A day or so later I shared the news with my pastor and asked for prayer. "But please don't publish this in the church bulletin," I asked, "since I am alone."

He quietly replied, "You are not alone."

I knew He was reminding me of the Lord's promise: *And surely I am with you always* (Matthew 28:20, NIV). But I felt so alone! I had felt this way ever since Ty's death.

The pastor went on. "Would you like someone to go with you?"

"No," I replied. "There are several procedures I have to undergo. I'll be in the hospital most of the day."

"The day" arrived right on schedule. The night before, when I opened my Bible for my daily Bible reading, I decided to turn to Psalms. I opened it and somehow turned to Psalm

20, and a word in the first verse caught my attention. "*May the Lord answer you when you are in distress . . .* " Distress! *I'm certainly in distress tonight*, I thought as I continued reading.

> *May the name of the God of Jacob protect you.*
> *May He send you help from the sanctuary and grant*
> *you support from Zion . . .May He give you the desire*
> *of your heart and make all your plans succeed.*
> Psalm 20:1, 2, 4 (NIV)

The words of the psalm were comforting.

At the hospital the next morning I was assigned a bed in Day Surgery.

Shortly after, I noticed a couple entering one of the booths across from mine. *Why, it's Peggy and Dan! I haven't seen them since they left the church. How long has it been? Five or six years?*

Peggy saw me and hurried over. "What are you doing here?" she asked. When I explained, the smile in her brown eyes faded, and concern slipped in. She chatted with me for a while before leaving. "But I'll be back," she said.

And she did return, accompanied by the pastor of her church, and they prayed with me. She stopped by again just before my surgery. "Dan's tests are finished, and we are leaving," she whispered, "but I wanted to say goodbye and wish you well." She smiled, squeezed my hand, and was gone.

Several hours later I left the hospital giving thanks to the Lord that everything went well and the cancer had been removed—and for Peggy and Dan. A little later, just before bed, I wanted to read Psalm 20 once again; it had been so comforting the night before. When I reached the second verse, I stopped—and simply stared at the words: *May He send you help from the sanctuary and grant you support from Zion.*

And just then the Lord said to me, "Isn't that what I did for you today?"

I was stunned. Memories of the morning, of Peggy and Dan, of their pastor and how they prayed with me, rushed into my head. And now the Lord was telling me that He was with me the night before and all through the day. He was telling me it was not a coincidence that Peggy and Dan had been there. The Lord had arranged things in this way. And I knew: never once had I been alone.

* * *

The breast cancer surgery took place in May 2011, just sixteen months after Ty's funeral. The diagnosis was a shock, for I thought, as many do, "Oh, that will never happen to me." But I learned that it can happen—and it does. And when it happened, I grumbled.

"Lord, all those times I was with Ty with his cancer diagnoses and treatments, and now I have to go through this alone?"

But the Lord helped me see that I was not alone. Not then, nor in the year to come.

Reflection

"Whoever has my commands and obeys them, he is the one who loves me. He who loves me will be loved by my Father, and I too will love him and show myself to him."
John 14:21 (NIV)

The author was astounded with how the Lord revealed to her that He was with her the night before her surgery and throughout the next day.

Has there been a time that, you now believe, the Lord revealed himself to you? A time when you could see how He was working in your life? Write about that time.

What effect did this have on you?

ONCE AGAIN

It was February 2012, and I was in the surgeon's office. Several days had passed since the recent biopsy.

"You have breast cancer," the doctor said.

What? Again! I had heard those exact words before . . .

Only nine months had passed since my first surgery with breast cancer. When I learned the devastating news the previous year, my spirits, already low as I was recovering from losing Ty, fell even lower. And now it was happening again—with the first experience still neon-bright in my ongoing battle.

In May 2011 I had undergone a lumpectomy for invasive breast cancer in the left breast. That surgery was followed a few weeks later with four to five weeks of radiation. Still healing from my grief over losing Ty, I spent a lot of time lying on the couch, my strength zapped by the treatments I was undergoing. And then, after the four to five weeks of radiation were completed, adjuvant therapy (hormonal treatment to help prevent the cancer from recurring) began.

With this second diagnosis the cancer was small, noninvasive *(in situ)*, and in the right breast. The news, coming so soon after the first experience, was definitely a surprise, but it felt different this time. This was the second go-round, and this time I knew what lay ahead. And, most important, this time my faith had been strengthened. Remembering Psalm 20, I *knew* I wasn't alone. But I didn't want it to be happening again! I wanted to survive.

When those of us who are breast cancer patients first hear those dreaded words—*"You have cancer"*—we become a member of an elite group, all hoping to survive and become part of the "five-year survivors club." It is reported that, statistically, if one's cancer is going to recur, it will be within the five-year period immediately following the diagnosis. We all hope to make it through those five years and become a member of the club!

But here I was in my second year following the first diagnosis—and already diagnosed for the second time. Again, the cancer was removed surgically with a lumpectomy. Since it was small and noninvasive, the team of doctors caring for me did not believe radiation was necessary. Nevertheless, it was still a cause for deep concern for me. Would I make it through the next five years? Would I be a survivor?

Reflection

When we lose someone we love, our life with that person immediately becomes a "yesterday." In the midst of our pain it is important that we remember our "yesterday."

Memories help keep that loved one close.

Suppose there had been no "yesterday." How would life have been different?

THROUGH THE YEARS
AND BEYOND

As I write these memoirs, a decade has passed since my second diagnosis of breast cancer in February 2012. Definitely, I qualify as a member of the Survivors' Club. To a breast cancer survivor, that feeling has to be equivalent with climbing Mount Everest or winning an Olympic gold medal. I have not only survived five years, but almost double that amount of time.

Moreover, during those years, in addition to surviving breast cancer, I have also, with the Lord's help, come a long way on my journey of grief.

But, as I have discovered, one of life's absolutes is surely this: we never know what lies ahead.

In October 2021, in the midst of the COVID-19 pandemic, I found myself back in the surgeon's office, for the third time hearing her words, "You have breast cancer." Once again I have been fortunate in that, although invasive, the cancer was discovered early and was small. Two weeks later, the cancer was removed through a lumpectomy. Nevertheless, it was disappointing to have to hear the diagnosis once again. I had so hoped that cancer would never again happen to me—but it had. However, with this third occurrence, having been through the experience twice, the news did not seem as devastating, for I knew what lay ahead—and I knew that I *could* be a survivor. After all, I had already survived, through the grace of God, not once, but twice. But to complicate matters this time, twelve days following my cancer surgery, my son passed away. It was his heart, sudden and unexpected. His death followed that of his wife Joan eight months earlier. And so . . . my journey continues.

I remember the moment, those many years ago during Ty's illness with Hodgkin's, when I first became familiar with the Scripture that says we should give thanks in all things. And how I balked at that idea. I just could not give thanks for Ty being so sick. But then I searched for the things I could give thanks for at the time, and I saw how the Lord was blessing us. And since then, through the years I have found that—in all things—God's loving hand is always present, reaching out to us, showing His love for us, bestowing His blessings upon us. In the good times and the bad.

Today I can thank the Lord for my time of grief, for it forced me to draw closer to Him. I do not know how I could have survived the awful pain of losing Ty without the Lord's help. I thank Him too that the experience has made me stronger. And I thank Him for all the people He sent into my life to help me each time I needed help. There are many other things to thank Him for, but the most important is that, as He has promised, He was always with me.

I have no doubt the Lord was there with Ty and me when we learned of his Hodgkin's. He was there, and He heard my frantic message, one very much like Mary's and Martha's: "Lord, one you love is sick." He was there the night I searched and searched the Scriptures for some word of hope, some word of comfort, and He sent His message: *You shall yet sing his praise.* The Lord was present with each radiation treatment Ty had to endure. He was present at the dinner table each time I had to run for the utility bucket. And without a doubt, I know He was there with me and my family in the funeral parlor that cold, wintry day in January. He was there in the cemetery as we stood beside the cold gray casket that held my husband's lifeless body. He was there in the hearse as we drove away. Yes, just as He was there for Mary and Martha those many centuries ago, He was there for me. And He is there for all who mourn.

As I write this today, again I am wondering: *Will I make it through the next five years and once again be a breast cancer survivor?* Only the Lord knows the answer. My life and my future are in His loving hands, and no matter what lies ahead, we have His promise.

> *God has said, "Never will I leave you; never will I forsake you" (Hebrews 13:5, NIV).*

The Lord has been a presence in all of my life. And He has been by my side from the very moment He called Ty home that cold, wintry Tuesday in December 2009. He walks with me. Never once have I walked alone.

Jesus said,
"Blessed are those who mourn,
for they will be comforted."

MATTHEW 5:4 (NIV)

FROM MY HEART TO YOURS

MODERN PSALMS
OF HOPE AND COMFORT

MORNING SONG

If I'm quiet enough,
and still,
I can almost hear the music all around;
in the rustle of the leaves on the maple trees,
in the dance of the branches on the pines
along the drive.
And when the morning breeze
ruffles my hair,
I feel the touch of Your hand, Lord,
and my heart sings Your praise,
attuned to the music
of the spheres.
This is Your world, Lord;
I know
You are near.

Shout for joy, O heavens; rejoice, O earth; burst into song,
O mountains! For the Lord comforts his people
and will have compassion on his afflicted ones.
Isaiah 49:13 (NIV)

THE MOURNER'S PSALM

My eyes fail, my tears are many;
I am in torment within
because the one I love is no longer.
Even so, the Lord is my Shepherd;
it is He who guides me. He walks with me
through the shadows in the valley
where death doth dwell; and He comforts me.
He will turn my sadness into joy,
for He has promised to prepare a place for me
and those I love, who trust in Him,
that where He is, we may also be.
I will trust in his unfailing love forever.

*Trust in the Lord with all your heart and lean not
on your own understanding; in all your ways acknowledge
him and he will make your paths straight.*
Proverbs 3:5, 6 (NIV)

ONLY GOD

When hearts are broken,
only You, Lord,
can soften those sharp jabs of pain
that block our sleep;
or ease the constant ache
within our hearts
that never goes away;
or take away the emptiness
that fills each hour
of each day,
without, within.

Only You.

In our midst,
You share our grief;
You see our broken hearts,
You hear our "Why?";
and tenderly You wait,
our pain to ease,
our hope restore.
Oh, so close,
ever nigh,

Only God.

Mary Emma Tisinger

I lift up my eyes to the hills—where does my help come from?
My help comes from the Lord, the Maker of heaven and earth.
Psalm 121:1, 2 (NIV)

EASTER BASKETS

Outside, winter lingers; the air is not so warm.
Is it the wind that adds the chill?

Children race across the lawn, searching
for treasures . . . hidden in the wee hours
by a huge white rabbit with long floppy ears and a
cotton-ball tail . . . while chocolate bunnies
and jelly beans danced in their dreams.
There will be time later for remembering the cross,
the old wooden cross
that stood high on Calvary's hill;
the cross on which our Savior, Jesus of Nazareth,
was crucified—and died—one day in spring,
long, long ago, when winter lingered.

The empty tomb took away the chill.

"He is not here; he has risen, just as he said.
Come and see the place where he lay."
Matthew28:6 (NIV)

NOT JUST A PIECE OF WOOD

I edge my way through the raucous crowd.
Is that a piece of wood I see,
rising up above the heads of those
who line the narrow street?
Closer, the noise diminishes;
the mood seems to change.
I see distress, even pain,
in the eyes of some who watch,
and then I see
Him.
He struggles,
staggering under the heavy load.
His brow is wet with perspiration;
His hair, matted with blood.
Why, it's Jesus, Jesus of Nazareth . . .
and He carries—not just a piece of wood—
but a cross,
the Cross of Calvary.

*Let us fix our eyes on Jesus, the author and perfecter
of our faith, who for the joy set before him endured the cross,
scorning its shame, and sat down at the right hand of the
throne of God.*
Hebrews 12:2 (NIV)

A PSALM OF PRAISE

Lord, You have promised
to be always with me;
my heart is filled with Your praise.
Your presence ever surrounds me . . .
In the misty light of the morning,
in the deep dark shadows of the night,
in evening's twilight haze, You are there.
I'm not alone.
Lord, there's no place void of Your spirit.
You're in the rose trailing over the railing,
in the ivy and the long-leaf pine,
in the beetle lumbering toward me . . .
I see Your power, Your presence, Your greatness;
and I rest in the shadow of Your wings.
Your name I will praise forever,
for You are with me;
I am never alone.

God is our refuge and strength, an ever-present help in trouble.
Psalm 46:1 (NIV)

THE MAPLES

There were two.
"Two maples," Tom said,

"for your new house and lawn."
That was twenty-two years ago.

Today the maples rise high,
high above the house.

With limbs outstretched
they reach for the stars.

I, too, reach for the stars,
with my limbs outstretched;

seeking just to touch, not the stars,
not the sun or the moon,

but the hem of His garment.
Seeking just to touch

the hand of the Master . . .
So that I can grow,

and soak up all the light,
the energy,

the essence of our Creator . . .
that my soul will hold.

*Blessed is the man who does not walk in the
counsel of the wicked . . . But his delight is in the law
of the Lord, and on His law he meditates day and night.
He is like a tree planted by streams of water . . .*
Psalm 1:1-3 (NIV)

YOU SPOKE

You spoke
and the earth was formed
the waters foamed
and the sun and the moon gave out their light

You spoke
the lion roared
the trees took root
and the lark and the dove soared into flight

You spoke, Lord,
and man was born
and into his form
You breathed Your breath—the breath of life

You spoke
the rains came down
the waters moved; Goliath fell
and a virgin gave birth in Bethlehem

Today You speak
to a world in strife
to a world in fear
in need of Your love, in need of Your peace
Lord, give us hearts . . . and ears to hear.

For he is our God and we are the people of his pasture,
the flock under his care. Today, if you hear his voice,
do not harden your hearts . . .
Psalm 95:7, 8 (NIV)

I WAIT

O Lord,
sometimes you seem so far away
my heart despairs

my cry of pain . . . My God, where are you?
You're nowhere to be found

I need to see your face
to hear your voice

to feel your gentle touch upon my head
upon my hand

I need to know, truly know
that you are near

that you are here
beside me

speak, Lord,
speak to my heart

I wait for the Lord, my soul waits,
and in his word I put my hope.
Psalm 130:5 (NIV)

WHAT MAN IS THIS

That night, in the boat
on the Sea of Galilee,
the winds died down
at the sound of Your voice
and the waters ceased
their swelling.

What manner of man is this?
they cried,

astonished by Your power as
they walked by Your side,
listened to Your voice,
and saw with their eyes

the miracles You performed
when You graced the earth
with Your presence.

And now, today, would that I
could walk by Your side,
sit at Your feet,
listen to Your voice,
and see the power of Your hand.

Then I too, Lord, would cry,
*What manner of man
is this?*

. . . the wind was against them. About the fourth watch of the night he went out to them, walking on the lake . . . when they saw him . . . they were terrified. Immediately he spoke to them and said, "Take courage! It is I. Don't be afraid." Then he climbed into the boat with them, and the wind died down. They were completely amazed.

Mark 6:48-51 (NIV)

IF I COULD

If I could, Lord,
I would walk by Your side
through the sand on the shore
by the Sea of Galilee
then climb into the boat
with Peter, Andrew, James, and John
and at Your command
do my best to become
a fisher of men

I would sit by Your side
and listen to Your voice
gentle and kind
yet filled with all power
and draw strength
from Your presence

and then, Lord, if I could
I would kneel at Your feet
like Mary Magdalene of old
let all the hurt, the pain, slip away
and bathe Your feet with my tears
tears of sadness
tears of joy

If only I could.

*As Jesus walked by the Sea of Galilee, he saw Simon and his
brother Andrew casting a net into the lake, for they were
fishermen. "Come, follow me," Jesus said, "and I will make
you fishers of men." . . . A little farther, he saw James son of
Zebedee and his brother John in a boat, preparing their nets.
Without delay he called them, and they
left their father . . . and followed him.
Mark 1:16-20 (NIV)*

FRUIT OF THE VINE

I am the vine,
you are the branches;
abide in me . . .

Those were Jesus' words
spoken to his disciples that last night
before He was arrested
in the Garden of Gethsemane.

His words, spoken on that day
to His disciples, speak today
to you and me.

Remain in me . . . Jesus said.
If a man remains in me and I in him,
he will bear much fruit . . .

like the fruit of the vine—
rich, succulent, fruity,
sweet to the tongue . . .

and even greater works
than I have done
you will do.
Abide in me.

Oh Lord,
hold me tight

and never let me go,
no matter how hard I strain
to pull away.

"I am the true vine, and my Father is the gardener.
He cuts off every branch in me that bears no fruit, while every
branch that does bear fruit he prunes so that it will be even
more fruitful. . . . Remain in me, and I will remain in you."
John 15:1-4 (NIV)

HEART-CRY

where are You, Lord
I long to see your face

I feel there is no place
for me to hide

to shelter from the storms
that swell around me

like ripples in the ocean . . .
like rolling waves

that drive the angry tides
why, Lord

why do troubles come
one after another

wind upon wind
rain upon rain

'til I am drenched
drowning in the torrents . . .

my vision blurred
my faith grown dim

strengthen me, Lord

help me be still

and wait for You

O Lord, hear my prayer, listen to my cry for mercy;
in your faithfulness and righteousness come to my relief.
Psalm 143:1 (NIV)

MY REFUGE

When thunder booms above the clouds,
the sky grows dark
and the wind increases speed;

when the leaves on the trees
do an inside-out,
and rain water floods the streets;

I need not fear . . .
for You, Lord,
are master of the storm,

of the night, of the day,
of the wind and the waves;
and I rest in the shelter of Your hand.

And when life grows hard,
the nights are long,
and the sun forgets to shine;

when my heart despairs,
and the tears won't cease,
I will remember, Lord,

You are master of the storm.
You are my rock, my refuge,
my peace.

I would hurry to my place of shelter,
far from the tempest and storm.
Psalm 55:8 (NIV)

ON THAT NIGHT

I wonder . . .
On that night, out in the fields
when all was quiet
and shepherds watched . . .
what hour it was
the angels sang their song
of peace on earth
good will to men?

I see . . .
a light so bright,
that even the snails
crawled out of their shells
and night owls grew still.
Did they know, could they tell
how great the event
of which the angels spoke?

Did the sheep awake?
And did they bleat
as the shepherds rubbed their eyes,
grabbed their staffs,
and to their knees they fell
in wonder and in fright
at the angels' words . . .

"For unto you is born this day
in a manger in Bethlehem,

a Savior, who is Christ the Lord.
His people He will save;
Jesus, Immanuel."

And there were shepherds living out in the fields nearby,
keeping watch over their flocks at night. An angel of the Lord
appeared to them, and the glory of the Lord shone around
them, and they were terrified. Suddenly a great company of
the heavenly host appeared with the angel, praising
God and saying, "Glory to God in the highest . . ."
Luke 2:8, 9, 13, 14 (NIV)

THE WORD

In the beginning was the Word
and the Word was with God
and the Word was God

and the Word became flesh
and dwelt among us
in a lowly manger in Bethlehem
while the angels sang
and wise men traveled from afar

And then one Sabbath
Jesus stood in the synagogue
and opened the scroll to read
from the prophet Isaiah

The Spirit of the Lord is upon me
because He has anointed me . . .
to bring good news to the poor

"And today," He said,
"these words are fulfilled
in your ears."

and The Word became flesh
and dwelt among them
The Word . . . living, breathing
. . . standing before them
and they knew Him not.

That which was from the beginning, which we have heard,
which we have seen with our eyes, which we have
looked at and our hands have touched—
this we proclaim concerning the Word of life.
1 John 1:1 (NIV)

TO YOUR PROMISES I CLING

Without Your love
I could not survive another hour,
another day.

Since a child
You have been a presence in my life,
unseen by human eyes,
Your voice unheard by human ears,
but present still.

And though I cannot look upon Your face
for the radiance there,
I can feel Your warmth, Your love,
Your presence near in prayer.

Come to me, You have said,
all you who are weary and heavy-laden.
Yoke with me, and learn of me,
and I will give you rest.

Such joy, such peace, in Your words I find;
words that were spoken in days of old
when heavenly feet touched earthly soil; yet

You are the same today
as You were then.
Forgive my doubt, my lack of faith.

Strengthen me, Lord.
To You, Your love, Your promises,
I cling.

"Come to me, all you who are weary and burdened, and I will give you rest. Take my yoke upon you and learn from me, for I am gentle and humble in heart, and you will find rest for your souls. For my yoke is easy and my burden is light."
Matthew 11:28-30 (NIV)

TOO NUMEROUS TO COUNT

Fresh every morning, Lord
Your blessings I see

blessings upon blessings
grace upon grace

through eyes dulled by tears
tears of sadness

of heartache, of pain
yet, by my side

steadfast, You remain
You pour out Your love

Your mercy, Your grace
blessings upon blessings

too numerous to count
these I receive, Lord

and humbly I bow . . .
in Your presence.

Because of the Lord's great love, we are not consumed,
for his compassions never fail. They are new
every morning; great is your faithfulness.
Lamentations 3:22, 23 (NIV)

TASTE AND SEE

O Lord,
Blessed is the man
whose roots grow deep
within the rich, lush soil
of Your Word.

Blessed is he
whose heart hungers and thirsts
to feed upon Your truths;
nourished he will be.
He will walk uprightly
in mercy and peace.

Sweeter than honey
drawn from the honeycomb,
more pleasing than manna
sent from above;
Your Word, everlasting,
satisfies the hunger
in my soul.

The Lord is good.
Taste, and see.

*The law of the Lord is perfect, reviving the soul. The statutes of
the Lord are trustworthy, making wise the simple. The precepts
of the Lord are right, giving joy to the heart. . . .*

*. . . The ordinances of the Lord are sure
and altogether righteous. They are more precious than gold,
than much pure gold; they are sweeter than honey,
than honey from the comb. By them is your servant warned;
in keeping them there is great reward.*
Psalm 19:7-9, 11 (NIV)

I AM . . .

In the wilderness Moses stood in awe
before the burning bush,
and the ground on which he stood
was holy ground.
And from that burning bush
You spoke, Lord,

Go, Moses, go;
go into Egypt and bring my people out.
My people . . . who are called by my name.

"And whom," Moses asked, "shall I say
is sending me?"
And You, Lord, replied: *I AM.*

I am the Lord your God.
I am, I was, I will always be.
Tell them I AM sent me.

Speak to me, Lord, from a burning bush . . .
on my knees, by my bed,
at the kitchen table,
behind the wheel in my car,
by the Rose of Sharon
that blooms outside my kitchen door.

Your voice, Lord, let me hear;
Your name affirm, Your presence near;

let me hear You say, *I AM* . . .
So that I may say to all I see,
"He is the Lord, He is my God,
He is the Great I AM . . .
and He strengthens me."

The Lord is my light and my salvation; whom shall I fear?
The Lord is the strength of my life.
Psalm 27:1 (KJV)

HIS HAND

It was His hand
that made the world,
the moon, the stars, the sun
to give us light.

It was His hand that formed the earth,
the trees, the flowers,
the grass that grows beneath our feet,
to give us food and beauty
day and night.

It was His hand through which
the stately beasts were formed,
the horse, the cow, the sheep, the goat;
that we might be enabled,
nourished, and survive.

It was His Hand that gave me shape
within my mother's womb;
His Hand that sent His Son
on Calvary's Hill to die
for me . . . for you;

that we might know the promise
of eternal life.
It is His Hand that loves me still;
His Hand
I will forever trust.

I will proclaim the name of the Lord.
Oh, praise the greatness of our God! He is the Rock,
his works are perfect, and all his ways are just.
Deuteronomy 32:3, 4 (NIV)

HE PAID THE DEBT

in the shadow of Gethsemane
and an old wooden cross
high on the hill of Calvary

in the echoes of pain
from the nails driven in
to his hands and his feet

and the sword
that pierced his side
the curtain that sets apart

the Most Holy Place
that day was broken, torn
so that now we may enter

on wings of faith
into God's presence
the Most Holy

it was a high price to pay
but, Lord, you paid it all
for me

*And when Jesus had cried out again in a loud voice, he gave up
his spirit. At that moment the curtain of the temple was torn
in two from top to bottom. The earth shook and the rocks split.
Matthew 27:50, 51 (NIV)*

BUT MARY KNEW

When Mary said to you, O Lord,
"They have no wine . . . "
at the wedding feast so long ago,
what did you think?

No miracles yet you had performed
and no one knew who you really were;
except . . . Joseph the Carpenter's son.
But Mary knew.

Did you wonder *why*
her words that day
at the wedding feast?
You must have, Lord, for you replied,
"Woman, what is this to you and me?
My hour has not yet come."

I wonder what the servants thought
when you gave the command
to fill the vats with water?
"Water, ha!" They must have scoffed . . .
"For a wedding feast? The guests want wine . . ."
But Mary knew.

"Do as He says . . . "
she said to them; and when they obeyed
it wasn't water the wedding guests drank
but the best of the fruit of the vine.

And most didn't know
it was the touch of Your hand, but . . .
Mary knew.

When he was twelve years old . . . they found him in the
temple courts, sitting among the teachers, listening to them
and asking them questions. Everyone who heard him was
amazed at his understanding and his answers . . . But his
mother treasured all these things in her heart.
Luke 2:42, 46, 47, 51 (NIV)

BLESS THE LORD

Bless the Lord, O my soul;
let everything within me
bless His holy name.

He hears my prayers,
my pleas for help,
for comfort, and for hope.

With David I will praise His name:
Jehovah God, the Great I Am;
my Rock, my Strength, my All.

I see the sun, the moon, the stars above;
how vast the universe, unsearchable,
reveals His power, His love.

I see Him in the lily white,
in the Rose of Sharon by my door,
in the robin nesting in the long leaf pine;
everywhere, His touch divine.

Bless the Lord, O my soul.
Let all that is within me
bless His Holy name.

*I will extol the Lord at all times; his praise will
always be on my lips. My soul will boast in the Lord,
let the afflicted hear and rejoice. Glorify the Lord with me;
let us exalt his name together.*
Psalm 34:1-3 (NIV)

A LIGHT ON A HILL

Lord, You called me to let my light shine
as on a hill—so all can see.

Sometimes, though,
that's not so easy to do;
as on those days
that come with disappointment . . .

those cloudy days
when the sun stays hidden;
or the rain pours down from your heavens
and the rivers rise;

or when the temperature drops
to an ice-cold level
and you never feel warm
no matter how thick your coat or sweater.

It's hard, Lord, on days such as these
to keep on shining,
to be that light on a hill
that brightens the lives of others.

Only with Your help, Lord,
will I be able
to keep my light glowing . . .
and reveal the way

to You.

*"You are the light of the world. A city on a hill
cannot be hidden. Neither do people light a lamp
and put it under a bowl. Instead they put it on its stand,
and it gives light to everyone in the house. In the same way,
let your light shine before men, that they may see your good
deeds and praise your Father in heaven."
Matthew 5:14-16 (NIV)*

ON BENDED KNEE

Lord, I wait
in silence now
on bended knee

I need . . .
I need . . .
I NEED . . .

Your voice to hear
that still, small voice
of love

O Lord
My God
hear my plea

let me feel Your touch
upon my head
upon my heart

touch all of me
show me how to live
teach me how to love

as You love me

"As the Father has loved me, so have I loved you.
Now remain in my love. If you obey my commands,
you will remain in my love . . . My command is this:
Love each other as I have loved you."
John 15:9, 10, 12 (NIV)

THE WOMAN AT THE WELL

Patiently He waited there
at the well
knowing she would come;
as was her custom at this hour . . .
to hide her shame
and avoid the scorn
of those who knew her way of life.
He waited there to offer her
a better way.

She saw Him sitting there
as she drew near, and wondered,
yet she had no fear.
A stranger would not know
her cause for shame.
'Twas then, He spoke.
"Give me a drink," He said.

"What! You—a Jew—
are asking me, a Samaritan,
for a drink of water?"

She did not know;
she *could not* know,
He was more than just "a Jew."
But as they talked
her eyes were opened
and she saw . . .

He was the Lord,
He was the Christ.

She gave him water from the well;
He gave her life.

*Jesus answered her, "If you knew the gift of God
and who it is that asks you for a drink, you would have
asked him and he would have given you living water."*
John 4:10 (NIV)

NOT MY FEET ONLY

In the upper room that day
You stooped down, Lord,
to wash the feet of your disciples.
But headstrong Peter balked . . .
appalled, he cried, "Not my feet, Lord,
You shall *not* wash *my* feet."

To which you solemnly replied,
"I must, Peter, or else
you have no part of me."
Abashed, poor Peter cried,
"Then, not my feet only, Lord,
wash my head; wash my hands . . .
cleanse all of me."

You stooped down, Lord,
that infamous night before Your arrest,
girded a towel around your waist,
and washed the dust from off the feet
of those who followed You—to show
that others we are to serve.

You spoke to me, as well, that night.
I heard your tender voice, I saw
your gentle touch, and though my dirty feet
rather would I hide . . . with my bunions,
callouses, and corns . . . I *must* have You.
With Peter then I gladly cry,

Not my feet only, Lord,
wash my head, wash my hands . . .
cleanse all of me.

"Now that I, your Lord and Teacher, have washed your feet,
you also should wash one another's feet. I have set you an
example that you should do as I have done for you."
John 13:14, 15 (NIV)

WHY, LORD?

Why is life so hard, Lord?
Flesh of my flesh and bone of my bone;
I weep for those I love.

I awake to the dawning sun
and for a brief moment my spirits rise,
and then I remember
that day in November . . .

He looked so peaceful lying there;
asleep, we thought;
but there was no response
when we called his name.

Or to my touch
upon his shoulder.
"The heartline's flat," the medics said.
"We're sorry, but he's gone."

Another cold November day.
Chilled . . . my heart.
We left the casket closed
for I could not bear
to see him there;
eyes shut, unseeing . . .

He could never see without his glasses.
Oh, my son, my son!

And the king was much moved, and went up to the chamber over the gate, and wept: and as he went, thus he said, "O my son Absalom, my son, my son Absalom! Would God I had died for thee, O Absalom, my son, my son!"
2 Samuel 18:33 (KJV)

HEARTLINE

'Tis only a line on a computer screen
measuring the heartbeat,
moving up and down and over;
and then again,

up and down and over.
Minute by minute,
hour by hour,
day by day;

in perfect rhythm,
continually . . .
marking the beat of our lives.
Until, unless,

the rhythm fails
and the beat, interrupted;
or it is no more
and the line grows flat.

Yet the screen doesn't show
the heartline continues;
no longer in need of an earthly beat,
it streams us back to the source
from which we came . . .

back to God.

"I will give them a heart to know me, that I am the Lord.
They will be my people, and I will be their God,
for they will return to me with all their heart."
Jeremiah 24:7 (NIV)

ACKNOWLEDGMENTS

When I began *I Did Not Want to Let You Go,* my goal was a book that would be of help to those who are grieving. During the process, however, the Lord changed my direction—He asked that I show how He has worked in my life. Hence, a change to the format of my book, and the subtitle, *A Widow's Walk with God.* First and foremost, then, I must express my gratitude to the Lord. He is my Source, my Strength, my Rock; I will praise His holy name forever.

I must also give a heartfelt thank you to my publisher, Larry Carpenter (Carpenter's Son Publishing), who took the time to meet with me at the Greater Philadelphia Christian Writer's Conference and discuss my book. He gave me excellent advice, which I have tried to follow. And to Shane Crabtree for his patient guidance and direction as we worked to get the book into print, editor Bob Irvin for the many hours he spent refining the manuscript, and Suzanne Lawing for her skillful design.

A word of gratitude is also due the Reverend Roland Coon (Calvary Assembly of God), who walks so closely with the Lord, for his review of the book for biblical and spiritual soundness. I am thankful for his encouragement. And to my grandson, Anthony Bogetti (University of Pittsburgh, Research Department), for his critical eye and helpful suggestions. And to my daughter Lisa, my sounding board, who lovingly sees that I keep my foot on the pedal: my grateful appreciation.

NOTES

PART II
1. *World Book Encyclopedia,* Volume 8, Field Enterprises Educational Association, USA, 1969, 169.

PART III
1. *World Book Encyclopedia,* Volume 9, Field Enterprises Educational Association, USA, 1969, 248.

2. *Dead Poets Society,* Peter Weir, director (TouchstonePictures/Silver Screen Partners IV; Buena Vista Pictures, distributor),1989.

PART V
1. The pastor read the words contained on two plaques at the funeral service. The first, "I asked God for all things . . . " is a quote by Alan Grant.

2. The poem on the second plaque, "That Man Is a Success," did not have an author's name listed; however, my research has shown this version is usually attributed to Robert Louis Stevenson. The poem has appeared in different versions, and there is some question as to the actual author. Some credit Bessie Anderson Stanley, others Ralph Waldo Emerson.

PART VI
1. The lists of things to do before and after the funeral were taken from lists supplied by Torbert's Funeral Services, Dover, Delaware.

2. Buechner, Frederick, *Now and Then* (San Francisco: Harper Collins Publishers,1983), 56.

3. Waters, Chris Ann, *Seasons of Goodbye* (Georgetown, Delaware: Fruitbearer Publishing, LLC, 2014), 65.

PART VIII
1. Amy Spencer, "The Eternal Sunshine of Liam Neeson," *Parade Magazine,* The Delaware State News, April 24, 2022.